Losing True North

Justin Trudeau's Assault on Canadian Citizenship

Candice Malcolm

ISBN: 978-0-9939195-1-0

To my husband, Kasra: the most patriotic Canadian I know.
He migrated to Canada from the Middle East when he was 12.

CONTENTS

PART 1: A CIVILIZATION ON THE BRINK

CHAPTER 1: SOCIETY AT WAR

ISLAMISTS V. THE WEST

It was a mild Friday evening in late autumn. David Nolan had surprised his girlfriend Katie Healy with a trip to Paris to celebrate her 28th birthday. As Audrey Hepburn's character in the movie Sabrina said, "Paris is always a good idea."

After a romantic dinner and drinks, the Irish couple made their way to a concert.

"It was a bit like Christmas already even though it was just November," he later told Sean Dunne of the Irish Daily Mail.[1] "We went to the Eagles of Death Metal concert and there was a nice relaxed atmosphere outside the Bataclan theatre before we went in."

The couple made their way inside the grand Parisian theatre and onto the dance floor. The show was barely underway when everything changed.

"All of the sudden this chaos started behind us. We heard what seemed like a scuffle and a load of banging. We thought people might have set off fireworks because there was sparks and rapid firing," he said to Dunne.

“I saw the silhouette of a man at the door but then with that first burst of gunfire, the crowd kind of fell to the side and it became quite clear that it was not fireworks at that point, and that it was gunfire. The reason these people had fallen was because they had been shot.

“People next to us had been shot,” David told the Daily Mail.

“I fell to the ground with Katie amongst the other bodies both alive and dead.

“We were both lying on the ground, but I was lying on top of Katie to protect her. And I could see the feet of this man. And it was clear he was dying. There was blood draining from his shoes. To my left there was a woman lying on the floor, and she was motionless. And then, it was clear, she was also dead. It seemed that everyone around us … was dead.

“At this point the gunman or gunmen [were] walking around shooting people individually because the burst of gunfire had stopped, and there now were single shots. And I could hear them away from me but also getting closer. At that point he, or whoever was shooting, was finishing people off.

“We both felt at that point that the [next] shot is going to be us.”

David lay on top of Katie, and the couple quietly said their goodbyes. He was worried that the bullets would tear through his body and kill his beloved Katie lying below.

“I remember seeing the gunmen, literally within feet of us.

“Again, somehow the bullets never came,” David Nolan told Sean Dunne of the Irish Daily Mail.

“He never pointed the gun at us. He walked past us and went up to the left of us — towards the bar area where I think he fired more shots.

“He was just randomly shooting people who were already dead or dying. It was kind of around that moment that I saw a set of doors burst open to my left.”

David and Katie knew they had to get out of that theatre. They decided to make a desperate run for it.

"We got up to run but there were dead bodies everywhere. The floor was slippery from the blood and we stumbled to get out the door. There was just carnage all around us. Other people also got up and ran out that door at that point.

"We got out onto the street and the sudden realization that I had been shot crept in," he told the Daily Mail.

David was shot in the foot, and it was now Katie's turn to save his life.

She dragged him several blocks away from the theatre with the help of kind and generous Parisians on the street. They brought him into an apartment and performed first aid and wrapped his foot. But they could not stop the bleeding. It would take half a dozen surgeries to fix the "pulverized" bones in his foot.

Back inside the Bataclan, three gunmen strapped with explosives continued their twisted raid.

Julien Pearce, a reporter for France's Europe 1 Radio who was attending the concert, described the attackers as "calm and determined." He told CNN they reloaded their weapons three or four times during the initial 20-minute killing spree.[2]

The attackers shouted "Allahu Akbar" — God is Great in Arabic — as they randomly fired their guns into the crowd and reportedly threw hand grenades at the concertgoers.

Across town, three terrorist accomplices had already targeted a sold-out crowd at the Stade de France. At 9:20 p.m., a friendly international soccer match between France and Germany was already underway when a loud explosion occurred outside. The players could be seen stopping and looking around on the field, before reluctantly continuing play.

The explosion had come from a suicide bomber. The man had tried and failed multiple times to enter the stadium. He was stopped and patted down by a security guard who discovered the suicide vest, causing the terrorist to run. A few seconds later, he detonated his vest, killing himself and an innocent bystander.

He was supposed to have entered the stadium, set off his bomb and triggered panicked crowds to exit onto the streets where two more bombers were waiting.

Instead, a second bomber blew himself up at 9:30 p.m. near the stadium, and, at 9:53 p.m., the third man walked towards a McDonald's restaurant and blew himself up.

Outside the Bataclan, three more terrorists were carrying out their own raid and targeting popular nightlife spots. At around 9:25 p.m., the terrorists arrived on rue Bichat in the 10th arrondissement (district). They began to shoot at people outside Le Carillon restaurant.

They then crossed the street and fired their assault weapons at people inside the restaurant Le Petit Cambodge. These men, too, were reportedly shouting "Allahu Akbar" as they carried out their grisly massacre. The assailants fled in a car with Belgian plates; 15 people were killed here and another 10 critically wounded.

Just five minutes later, one of the gunmen burst into Café Bonne Bière further along rue Bichat, gunning down diners and killing five people.

His two accomplices fired their Kalashnikov rifles into an outdoor terrace of Le belle équipe on rue de Charonne. Nineteen people were killed, and nine more were left in critical condition.

The gunmen then escaped in their vehicle, including the suspected ringleader of the whole massacre, Abdelhamid Abaaoud. It would take French authorities five days to find this man — hidden in a flat just a few blocks from the Stade de France. He was killed after a long gun battle with police.[3]

At 9:40 p.m., one man walked into the Comptoir Voltaire café along the lively boulevard Voltaire in the 11th arrondissement. He sat down at a table, and placed an order with the waiter, and, a few minutes later, he detonated a suicide bomb that ripped the café apart. The man killed himself and injured 15 people, one severely.

Back inside the Bataclan, the attackers were still engaged with police. After the initial 20-minute killing spree, which left dozens dead, the terrorists took 100 hostages as police surrounded the concert hall.

The terrorists forced hostages to stand in front of doors and windows to provide a "human shield." They phoned police on the phone and spoke to a negotiator. The terrorists reportedly said "what you are doing in Syria, you are going to pay for it now" and "this is because of all the harm done by [French President François] Hollande to Muslims all over the world."[4]

They threatened to decapitate one hostage every five minutes and throw the corpse out the window.

According to survivors, one terrorist hopped onstage and began playing the xylophone while laughing manically at the petrified audience.[5]

For more than two hours, an intense standoff ensued.

Benjamin Cazenoves was one of those hostages, and he took to Facebook to describe the scene.[6] At 11 p.m., he posted in French, into what roughly translates to: "I'm still at the Bataclan. Top floor. Hurt Bad! It happened so fast. There are still some survivors inside. They are slaughtering everyone. One by one. Top floor soon!"

Some 25 minutes later, he posted again: "Alive. Just cuts … Carnage … Dead bodies everywhere."

By midnight, there were reports on social media that the terrorists had started killing hostages. An elite tactical unit of the Paris police finally launched an assault against the terrorists to save the remaining hostages.

One terrorist was shot, the other two detonated their suicide vests.

The massacre had finally ended.

David and Katie survived, and are now engaged — although David may have to go down the aisle in a wheelchair.

Benjamin Cazenoves also made it out of the Bataclan with only minor injuries.

But there were 89 people at the Bataclan who weren't so lucky.

In total, 130 souls were taken from Paris that mild evening of November 13, 2015. They were murdered, in cold blood, in a war they wanted no part of — a war they probably didn't even realize they were a part of.

Nine deranged Islamic terrorists forever changed one of history's greatest cities. They waged war against innocent civilians. They murdered men and women, young and old, locals and visitors, and targeted the places Parisians love the most — cafes, restaurants, the theatre, and a major sporting event.

They struck at the heart of our western civilization, in a city that has long represented beauty, and love.

But following this massacre, things changed. Paris's café culture retreated and fear set in.

It's easy to change your Facebook profile picture to the Eiffel Tower or tweet #JeSuisParis, but it's much more challenging to go back to the way things were. It's impossible to enjoy a meal at your favourite restaurant, when you're constantly looking over your shoulder and jumping at every sound.

It's even more difficult to try to make sense of the massacre, or come to terms with what it represents for Europe and the West.

These terrorists were not foreign agents. The attacks were carried out by French and Belgian nationals.

The nine men responsible were all the children of Muslim migrants, they all lived in isolated Muslim communities, they all became radicalized in Europe, and they all spent time in Syria fighting alongside Daesh, or the Islamic State. Several of them were being monitored by police and some had even been arrested, and let go, for suspected terrorist activities.

Two of the attackers were later found to have registered as refugees in Greece months earlier. One of the men was carrying a Syrian passport when he blew himself up.

Hearing these vivid accounts, reading about these savage killers and the damage they inflicted in just a few minutes one autumn evening, many Canadians were brought back to our own encounter with deadly Islamic terrorism.

Just one year earlier, we faced the same evil on a thankfully much small scale.

On a sunny Wednesday morning in October, a deranged radical Islamist struck Canada's capital in Ottawa. Shortly before 10 a.m., 32-year-old Michael Zehaf-Bibeau arrived at the National War Memorial carrying a stolen hunting rifle.

Canadian Forces Cpl. Nathan Cirillo was ceremonially standing on guard, symbolically carrying an unloaded weapon, at the Tomb of the Unknown Soldier. The monument represents Canadians who died in wars defending our freedom.

The terrorist approached 24-year-old Cirillo from behind and, at close range, shot him three times in the back. As Cirillo lay dying, two other soldiers on sentry duty tried to stop Zehaf-Bibeau, but he shot at them too, forcing them to scramble for safety.

Heyden Trenholm, an advisor for Northwest Territories Senator Nick Sibbeston, witnessed the attacks from a few feet away. He told a CBC reporter that after shooting the soldier in the back, the terrorist pulled down the scarf that was covering his face, raised the gun over his head and shouted "For Iraq!"[7]

Zehaf-Bibeau then retreated to his car parked beside the War Memorial and drove half a block to the gated entrance of Parliament Hill. There, he abandoned the car and continued on foot. Getting only halfway towards the Parliament building, he hijacked a cabinet minister's car, forcing the driver to jump out at gunpoint, and drove up to the entrance of Centre Block.

The radical Islamist then stormed into the Parliament building through an entrance beneath the Peace Tower.

He shot a security guard on his way in, and ran down the Hall of Honour towards the Library of Parliament straight ahead.

The terrorist planned his attack at the exact moment when all Members of Parliament hold their weekly caucus meetings.

Rifle in hand, the terrorist ran straight down the hallway and past the doorways to the meeting rooms.

Had he turned either left of right, he would have found a room full of either NDP or Conservative MPs, and sitting at the front of each room, either Opposition Leader Thomas Mulcair or Prime Minister Stephen

Harper.

Instead, the terrorist ran straight ahead, likely confusing the grand library entrance for the office of the prime minister. At the entrance, Zehaf-Bibeau was shot dead by the heroic sergeant-at-arms of the House of Commons, retired police chief Kevin Vickers, who happened to keep a sidearm in his office. Zehaf-Bibeau was shot 31 times by six officers, ending his deadly rampage.

It was a devastating attack, but it could have been much worse.

Back at the War Memorial, Nathan Cirillo was struggling to stay alive.

Master Cpl. Kyle Button, who was on roving sentry duty that morning, was the first to his side and began administering first aid.[8] He called for help and several heroic Canadians rushed to assist in any way they could. Despite the sheer terror caused by the shooting, and uncertainty about whether the attack was over or if the gunmen was acting alone, six people jumped to Cirillo's aid.

Barbara Winters, a lawyer and former naval reservist, was the second to Cirillo's side. She told CBC radio that she simply tried to comfort the wounded soldier while others tried to save his life. "I told him he was loved. And that he was brave. And that he was a good man," Winters said through tears.[9]

Cirillo was taken to a nearby hospital, where he succumbed to his wounds. The 24-year-old left behind a young son and loving family.

The city of Ottawa remained on lockdown for the rest of October 22, 2014, and the country began to mourn the death of a brave and loyal Canadian soldier. Canada experienced a terrifying and deadly terrorist attack on our home soil.

Another plot two days earlier also resulted in the death of a member of the Canadian Forces.

Martin Couture-Rouleau, a radicalized Quebecer and Muslim convert, had intentionally rammed his car into two Forces officers. Warrant Officer Patrice Vincent died from his injuries, and the terrorist was later killed in a shootout with police.[10]

Just as in Paris, Canada was suddenly thrust into a global war. Radical Islamic terrorists were in Canada, and were directing their fury at our servicemen.

A once-foreign war was now being launched against Canadians and members of our armed forces.

But Canadians showed their resolve.

They packed the Highway of Heroes — a stretch of Highway 401 between Trenton and Toronto — to honour the fallen soldiers. Canadians paused to reflect upon those who defend our country and protect our freedom.

Canadians from coast to coast and of every background began donating to a fund set up for the families of the victims,[11] with donations as small as $5 and as large as $50,000. In the letters they wrote alongside their donations, Canadians expressed feelings of helplessness, vulnerability and a desire to do more.

Terrorists strive to make us feel hopeless and afraid. By coming together and moving forward as a nation, wiser and more alert to the threats we face, we can deny terrorists of this satisfaction.

But we cannot deny that there is war and that we are a part of it.

Terrorists target civilians, meaning we have all been drafted to the front lines of this war. We can ignore these facts, and pretend this violence is simply the result of a mental illness or drug abuse, but that will not make us any safer.

The reality is that these Islamic terrorists are driven by a ferocious ideology and a deadly desire to conquer. Much like the fatal ideologies of the 20th century — fascism and communism — these jihadists fiercely believe in their cause and are willing to kill for it.

The West must recognize that we are at war with radical Islamic terrorists, motivated by a poisonous ideology. Rather than excuse these killers as deranged loners and petty criminals, we should look at their ideology, examine their behaviour and scrutinize those responsible for radicalization. We must better understand the enemy in order to better defend ourselves against it.

While Europe Slept

In Europe, the enemy is inside the gate. Twenty-first century modern warfare is being waged on multiple fronts and through multiple domains.

Meanwhile, Europe's docile leaders struggle to get basic facts straight as they come to terms with the problems brewing within.

Most of Europe's politicians have yet to summon the courage to name the enemy or identify its motive. Instead, they fall back on a vague and undescriptive term, "terrorism," and insist these "terrorists" have nothing to do with the religion they claim to be fighting for.

Europe's leaders dither about how to react, deny the religious ideology behind the attacks and shed tears in solidarity while their citizens are brutalized and slaughtered in unprovoked attacks.

Europe's leaders would rather blame Europeans themselves than admit that it is radical Islamists who are driving this war.

This enemy has disguised itself within Europe's distinct Muslim populations and hidden away inside the closed communities of Europe.

Security forces and political leaders are no longer dealing with a few isolated Islamic terrorists; they have a full-blown insurgency on their hands. Massacres and acts of war in Paris and Brussels —where three suicide bombers struck the airport and a train station, killing 32 and injuring 316 on March 22, 2016 — are a glimpse into what Daesh (also known as the Islamic State) has in store for Europe.

The wrath of the world's radical Islamist organizations is directed at liberal and progressive Europe, while key European liberal and progressive leaders continue to bend over backwards to accommodate those who actively plot to do them harm.

Europe's leaders are dealing with a crisis they themselves fueled through haphazard and ill-advised migration and integration policies, combined with a continued culture of denial.

While European leaders were trying in vain to adhere to state-led multiculturalist utopias, their continent has been transformed into a fractured and broken society.

The Brussels neighbourhood of Molenbeek is a prime example of Europe's transformation. This poor, disenfranchised and majority Muslim neighbourhood has become an underground network for Islamic terrorism.

Both the November 2015 Paris massacre and the March 2016 Brussels bombings were planned from Molenbeek and carried out, in part, by men born and raised in this neighbourhood.[12]

One of the architects of the Paris massacre, Saleh Abdeslam, was finally captured in Molenbeek just days before the Brussels bombings. For more than four months, this Daesh agent was harboured and supported by a network of jihadists; Abdeslam was finally arrested just a few blocks from the home where he grew up.[13]

Imagine the extensive network required to harbour this infamous murderer for more than 18 weeks — 128 days, to be exact. His photograph was plastered all over train stations, social media sites and the evening news. Yet, he was able to evade the combined security and policing authorities of the European Union. While on the lam, Abdeslam was able to travel freely, work with his network in Molenbeek and plan more attacks. He even had a hand in planning the Belgium bombings — perpetrated just three days after his arrest.

The Molenbeek terror cell is not alone. Hidden away in closed communities like Molenbeek, terrorists are able to plan attacks, smuggle weapons, establish safe houses and escape routes and move freely throughout their neighbourhood.

Migrant Muslims have been left to set up parallel societies; there are now hundreds, possibly thousands, of neighbourhoods in cities across the continent known as "no-go zones." Police refuse to enter and non-locals are encouraged to avoid them for their safety.

These communities are beset with social problems, ranging from illiteracy and unemployment, to gang violence and high crime rates. Amidst the poverty, boredom and disaffection, many become susceptible to a poisonous ideology. Radical Islam is peddled by recruiters in fundamentalist mosques that fill the role both of neighbourhood religious site and community centre.

Most people within these closed communities are not terrorists or religious extremists. Yet, there is a willingness among some to shelter fugitive terrorists and adapt to the growing radicalism within their community.

Security and intelligence officials are simply overwhelmed, unable to track the thousands of jihadists and returned foreign fighters dispersed throughout Europe.

Europe's border patrol agency, Frontex, released a report in April 2016 detailing the terrifying security dilemma Europe now faces. The report admits that jihadi terrorists are using the migrant crisis to enter Europe and says there are now a "staggering number" of radical Islamists in Europe.

Security officials are scrambling to keep up with the flow of terrorists, including many who are European citizens.

Intelligence agencies and police have been forced to admit their failure to keep track of all the jihadists pouring into Europe, let alone stopping them from orchestrating more attacks.

Terrorists are outsmarting officials and taking advantage of Europe's incompetence. Meanwhile, civilians are forced to live on the front lines of this war.

The security crisis in Europe has been decades in the making. It was caused by a series of political miscalculations. Europe's desperate and at times contradictory immigration policies have given rise to an integration crisis.

Continental integration policies, including the black magic potion of state multiculturalism, have permitted isolated Muslim communities, thereby giving rise to the creation of closed societies.

Europe's leaders stood by idly, even approvingly, as Muslim migrant communities self-segregated and set up these parallel societies, often governed by Sharia law.

Leaders within these closed communities increasingly reject western liberal values and instead promote religious fundamentalism and the myth of victimization of Muslims at the hands of secular Europeans.

Jihadists have been able to frame the battle of ideas and foster an environment that recruits angry young Muslims, and converts them into violent extremists.

Europe's leaders, led by German Chancellor Angela Merkel, have become embroiled in a quest for redemption, and have sought to redeem themselves through further reckless migration.

Consequently, millions of refugees have been given a no-string-attached invitation into the continent. And the world's aspirational migrants have taken Europe up on this offer. There were 1.82 million illegal border crossings in 2015, smashing the previous year's record by 600 per cent. That works out to about 5,000 migrants entering Europe each and every day. And there is no sign this tidal wave of migrants will slow down any time soon.

But Europe's leaders are doing no favour to these migrants or to their own citizens with this open invitation. The sheer logistics of dealing with such large numbers of migrants are incredibly complicated and time consuming.

Aside from requiring such basic life necessities as food, water and shelter, many migrants arrive suffering from acute illnesses, exhaustion, post-traumatic stress disorder, culture shock and facing a language barrier that makes the situation even more difficult.

Europe does not have the resources to provide these vast services to millions of migrants. Consequently, many newcomers end up living in squalor, unable to work or provide for themselves and contributing to the breakdown of law and order. And this is just the beginning of Europe's troubles.

Politicians throughout the continent continue to deny the sectarian violence being brought in alongside some migrants, and accuse anyone who raises concerns about this unrestrained migration of being a right-wing nationalist.

Any debate over immigration, integration and national security has been stifled. And while the political discourse has been paralyzed, jihadists are moving in and staging more attacks. Security forces have been caught flat-footed and are proving themselves vastly underprepared — incapable and incompetent — in dealing with the thousands of radical Islamists ready to wage war upon Europe.

Each mistake and its corresponding correction have managed to make the problem worse. Europe is in shell shock; citizens are angry, communities are divided, elites are in denial — even covering up crimes rather than coming to terms with the consequences of open borders — and the enemy is gaining ground.

There is a growing hostility between isolated Muslim communities and the broader European society; both sides are increasingly nervous and anxious about when the jihadists will strike next. Catastrophic political failures have created the largest threat to the security of Europe since the Second World War.

EUROPE'S CATASTROPHIC MIGRATION POLICIES

> "How did you go bankrupt?"
> "Two ways. Gradually, then suddenly."
>
> - Ernest Hemingway, The Sun Also Rises

To answer the question of how Europe got to this point, and what lessons we can take to prevent the rise of no-go zones in Canada and other western liberal democracies, we should look no further than Europe's migration policies over the past half-century. After all, the closed communities and no-go zones did not pop up overnight; they were formed over decades through Europe's lackadaisical migration policies. The problem built up gradually, then suddenly exploded through Europe's decision in 2015.

Europe's cataclysmic migration policies rose out of the aftermath of the Second World War. Europe's leaders were desperate to rebuild the continent. They faced intense labour shortages due to the substantial loss of life caused by the war, especially of young males. Western European nations signed labour migration agreements with southern European, North African and Middle Eastern countries.[14]

Western European nations sponsored millions of "guest workers" to work in the so-called 3D jobs — dangerous, dirty and dull — in mining, building, and transportation. They recruited young Muslim men in bilateral agreements with Turkey, Algeria and Arab countries from the former British Mandate.[15]

Large numbers of Turkish nationals arrived in Germany and, for the most part, these individuals were denied citizenship and access to Germany's democratic institutions.

Europe's migration policies were simply not based on reality. The broad expectation was that guest workers would eventually return to their nation of origin.

These migrants, however, had ideas of their own. They grew roots in their host countries; they settled down, got married, had families, built mosques and began to self-segregate into isolated diaspora communities. These ethnic communities began to grow, having large families and sponsoring more family members just as Europe's native population continued to decrease.

Through family reunification policies, Europe imported large numbers of migrants with no language skills or workplace qualifications, leaving significant portions of migrant communities dependent on Europe's generous welfare programs.[16]

In Denmark, for instance, immigrants receive 18 per cent of social benefit dollars despite only making up only three per cent of the population.[17]

Family reunification gradually replaced the guest worker programs and Europe found itself welcoming even larger numbers of unskilled and uneducated migrants. In Belgium, family reunification began to account for nearly 50 per cent of overall immigration.[18]

With Europe's immigration strategy lacking any economic considerations, migrant communities became further isolated and removed from host populations. In Germany, for instance, 14 per cent of the migrant population (defined by the German government as either a migrant or the descendant of a migrant who entered the country after 1950) lack school qualifications, compared to 1.8 per cent of non-migrants, and 43 per cent lack professional qualifications compared to 19 per cent of the native population.[19]

Both Canadian and American Muslim populations achieve rates of education and employment similar to those in the overall population.[20] This is simply not the case with European Muslims.

Europe's leaders did not foresee that these guest workers would stay, and thus, never devised a strategy to integrate them. In Germany, as in the rest of Europe, citizenship is handed down through blood rather than soil. Children born to guest workers were not granted citizenship. Consequently, there are now large swaths of third-generation migrants — the grandchildren of the original guest workers — who do not speak German and do not have German citizenship.[21]

Under the spell of state-enforced multiculturalism, Europe's leaders took a hands-off approach to integration. In this sense, multiculturalism is not a synonym with diversity or pluralism. It is a deliberate policy, employed by misguided liberals, that says newcomers can move to a new country and not change anything about themselves, their culture or community. They don't need to learn a new language, abide by the norms and values of the host society or even necessarily follow local laws. Every culture is equal, and host societies should remain neutral to cultures and values.

Not wanting to "impose" western values or culture upon newcomers, and imagining these migrants were only temporarily in Europe, host societies failed to engage or integrate them. Guided by cultural relativism and western guilt, elites in Europe insisted that migrants be able to maintain their own cultural identities.

Accordingly, newcomers by and large were never asked to learn the local language, study European history, respect the laws or observe the customs of the host society. They were never asked to interact with their neighbours, get to know people from other backgrounds, or engage in civic activities. Not surprisingly, the migrants resisted change. Many rejected liberal secularism and pluralism of Europe and instead abided by their own illiberal religious codes. They were left to form their own civil society and establish parallel communities hidden away from mainstream Europe.

By late 2010, many politicians could see the writing on the wall and began to finally see the error of their ways. Both Britain's David Cameron and Germany's Angela Merkel renounced multiculturalism, calling it a failed experiment.[22]

Europe could no longer simply ignore newcomers or follow the progressive liberal doctrine that prevented host societies from "imposing" anything upon newcomers.

However, engulfed in a culture of denial, these leaders have yet to set a new course of action or devise a realistic plan for welcoming and integrating newcomers.

Unfortunately, the damage to Europe has already been done.

Closed communities have fostered what cultural anthropologist and war photographer Teun Voeten calls, "a very deep, and very dangerous, undercurrent of radical Islamism."[23]

Voeten lived in Molenbeek for nearly a decade, but left after the community degenerated into an intolerant breeding ground of crime and radicalism. The self-described human rights advocate who frequently champions left-wing causes said he could "no longer stand to live in [a] despondent, destitute, fatalistic neighbourhood."

Europe's terrible immigration policies created unfathomable societal woes. But the reaction to the admitted failure of state multiculturalism once again made the problem worse.

Europe blamed itself for poor migration policies, and considered Muslim migrants to be only the victims of social and economic exclusion. Racked with guilt, Europe turned a blind eye to the growing problems permeating many Muslim communities.

In just five years since the condemnation of state multiculturalism, Europe's Muslim enclaves have become increasingly homogeneous, conformist and intolerant to outsiders.

Neighbourhoods in North London became unofficial "Sharia Zones" — patrolled by self-appointed moral police. Local supermarkets and shops stopped serving alcohol, cafes and restaurants segregated by religion, Jews were made increasingly unwelcome and gays were harassed by local gangs. These problems were routinely ignored by the elites and a culture of denial set in.

By 2015, Europe was a powder keg just waiting for a match. And the match was struck in the form of an open invitation to millions of refugees. As throngs of migrants from the Middle East marched across

Europe, they mostly headed towards countries with generous welfare programs and lenient policies towards asylum seekers — namely Germany, Britain and Scandinavian countries. Many others settled in locations with large diaspora communities — France, Belgium and the Netherlands.

Migrants and refugees joined the existing Muslim enclaves and exacerbated the problems that were hidden in plain sight. Far from dealing with the underlying problems of closed communities and a ruptured society, Angela Merkel's open-border policy magnified this internal crisis and further widened the divisions that were established over decades.

While they recognize the problem of closed communities, members of the progressive elite still dominate the discussion and decision-making regrading mass migration.

These elites cannot bring themselves to criticize the Islamists who are using Europe's closed Muslim communities as incubators for radicalization and terrorism. Instead, they maintain that Europe itself is to blame: anyone who raises concerns over the high crime rates, troubling intolerance and growing presence of jihadists within Muslim communities is just a racist to be condemned and ostracized.

The debate is further paralyzed by a perverse paternalism toward Muslims. Regardless of their ideology or possible hatred towards Europe, they are considered victims.

This may sound like a caricature of clueless leftist elites. If only it were an exaggeration.

"Who knows what horrors he has been through?" said Sweden's national police chief of a Somali migrant teenager accused of murdering his social worker.

The 22-year-old woman was stabbed to death at a migrant welcome centre, and yet, the chief publicly sympathized with her alleged killer. "Well, you are of course distraught on behalf of everyone involved …. Naturally, for the person killed and her family, but also for a lone young boy who commits such a heinous incident," said the chief.[24]

Naturally.

Leaders have cemented as fact the bizarre notion that radical Muslims are victims, both of exclusion at the behest of policy makers and racism in the modern political discourse.

Radicalized Islamists and violent migrants flooding into Europe are not the problem, they insist; the problem is racism and so-called "Islamophobia." If we just showed more compassion and sympathy, all the problems would disappear. This loose grasp on reality by the political elite has become increasingly evident. And everyday Europeans are rejecting this narrative. They are revolting against the elites and throwing their weight behind a rising anti-immigration political movement.

Europe's Muslim leaders have also had a hand in perpetuating dangerous myths. They have accepted that Europeans are to blame for the problems facing their communities. Many would rather maintain this narrative than work to combat crime, unemployment and radicalization within their own communities.

Europeans, of course, are not responsible for the rise of Islamic terrorism and violence around the world. They are not to blame for Islamist extremism, which is, after all, an ideological feud, not a grievance-based conflict.

Europe's leaders are, however, responsible for allowing terrorist outfits to infiltrate their communities and establish terrorist cells throughout Europe.

European leaders are to blame for not having the courage to address the problem or stand up against it.

Europe has made its bed, and it must now lie in it. The rest of the world, and particularly western liberal democracies with open migration systems such as Canada and the U.S., must learn from these catastrophic failures.

TRUDEAU'S CALCULATION

Looking at the crisis in Europe, we need to ask: is Canada heading in that direction?

In his first few months in office, Canada's Prime Minister Justin Trudeau was already unwittingly following in the footsteps of naïve and ill-advised European policymakers. Will the crisis befalling Europe arrive on our doorsteps in the years and decades to come?
The answer to these questions will depend upon decisions being made in Ottawa in 2016.

Canada has historically taken a different approach to immigration than our European counterparts. Our system has been more selective, more focused on economic success. Our approach to integration is far more deliberate. We ask newcomers to learn our language and engage with the broader community. We insist that newcomers respect our laws. And our borders are monitored, patrolled and secured.

Yet Justin Trudeau seems willing to discard these advantages in exchange for some cheap political points.

Trudeau is already taking a reckless approach to immigration and integration — fast-tracking migration from the midst of an active war zone, granting citizenship to convicted terrorists, eliminating the test for many new immigrants and giving away health care and social welfare benefits to the elderly parents and grandparents of new immigrants.

These policies sacrifice Canada's best interests and put our national security in jeopardy. Trudeau's Liberal government is dismantling Canada's Citizenship Act and putting the Liberal party's 2019 election planning ahead of our national security interests.

Trudeau's government is actively — deliberately — weakening the value of Canadian citizenship. He is flooding the country with unprecedented levels of immigration with one simple goal in mind: importing one million new citizens, one million new Liberal voters, in time for the next federal election.

Electoral politics aside, the unintended consequences of these rash immigration policies will have a devastating long-term impact.

Just as in Europe, Trudeau's progressive "sunny ways" are blinding him to the real threat posed by radical Islamist war-mongers; no number of hugs and hashtags will soften their desire for a holy war.

Trudeau is intentionally taking advantage of Canada's generosity and openness when it comes to welcoming newcomers, and naïvely making us vulnerable to attacks on Canadian soil. He is deliberately manipulating Canada's immigration policies for political gain as he leads Canada down the path of failed European migration policies.

Trudeau has learned nothing from the crisis in Europe. He is taking cues from European progressives and taking Canada down Europe's failed path. Trudeau is engaged in the same guilt-ridden preoccupation with coddling jihadists rather than speaking out against radicalism and empowering reformers within Muslim communities.

Europe's leaders have made catastrophic mistakes, and Trudeau is proudly following suit. He is pushing Canada's immigration system away from practical economics-driven nation building and towards Europe's failed approach of prioritizing family reunification and refugees.

When it comes to integration, Trudeau again is following Europe's failed example of resettlement, embracing the cult of official multiculturalism and ignoring the difficult work of integrating and engaging new immigrants in mainstream Canadian culture.

Trudeau is more concerned with reducing the so-called "barriers" to becoming a Canadian citizen and fast-tracking citizenship for newcomers than protecting all Canadians from the ongoing threat of murderous jihad.

Trudeau is more interested in gloating about his self-promoting and artificial pledge to accept as many as 50,000 Syrian refugees. He is less interested in demonstrating to Canadians that his government isn't taking any national security shortcuts.

While Trudeau is busy taking selfies and doing puff-piece interviews, Islamists are taking advantage of our generous immigration system and infiltrating North America, just as they did while Europe slept.

Why I Say Daesh

As I was working on this book, I got into a friendly debate with a friend who took issue with my using the term "Daesh" rather than the Islamic State, IS, ISIS or ISIL to describe the Islamic militant group. Apparently, in the U.S., Barack Obama's Secretary of State John Kerry is just about the only person to call it Daesh. In response, some have called it "cowardly" to use the term.

As painful as it is to say, in this instance, John Kerry is right.

Just like ISIS (Islamic State of Iraq and al-Sham, which can also roughly mean Islamic State of Iraq and Syria) or ISIL (Islamic State of Iraq and Levant), Daesh is an acronym, taken from the Arabic name for the group — Dawlat al-Islamiyah f'al-Iraq w belaad al-Sham. Da-I-I-Sh, or Daesh.

There are three major reasons I use Daesh. None of them fall in line with the leftist cowardice, or fear of offending people by calling this group "Islamic."

First, the terrorists hate it. Daesh sounds similar to the Arabic word "daes," which means "one who crushes something underfoot," or "dahes," which translates to mean, "one who sows discord." In fact, the terrorists hate it so much, they have banned it.

This is from an AP story in September 2014: "Several residents in Mosul, Iraq's second-largest city which fell to the extremist group in June, told The Associated Press that the militants threatened to cut the tongue of anyone who publicly used the acronym Daesh, instead of referring to the group by its full name, saying it shows defiance and disrespect."

Second, Conservative international leaders and security experts alike use the term Daesh. Australia's Tony Abbott, Britain's David Cameron and just about everyone in the Middle East uses the word. During my recent travels through the Middle East — Israel, Jordan, the West Bank and Syria — folks in the region that I spoke with unanimously used the term Daesh. Politicians, journalists, academics, activists, security officials and citizens alike all said Daesh. Are they cowards too?

Finally, we don't call other Islamic terrorist groups by an English translation of their propagandist names. No one calls Hamas "the Resistance" or al-Qaeda "the Foundation." No one calls Hezbollah "the Party of God." We use their Arabic names, which are often acronyms based on the idealistic names they give themselves. These fascist thugs may fancy themselves as martyrs and religious warriors, but we shouldn't dignify them by adopting their branding identity.

Daesh is a fledgling group with global aspirations. After the group's attacks in Europe and its crusades into Libya, Afghanistan and beyond, it no longer makes sense to think about its geographic territory as simply Iraq and Syria (or al-Sham or the Levant). Daesh largely operates online, so using a name based on geographic territory stood on shaky ground to begin with.

The other descriptive words "Islamic" and "state" are both loosely applicable. The group aspires to be both Islamic and a state. Despite their religious code and Qur'anic inspiration, many Muslims take issue with Daesh being considered "Islamic." Despite their bureaucracy and governing apparatus, most scholars would not consider it a state according to our Westphalian system, but instead consider it a non-state actor and terrorist group. Both of these concepts should be open for debate.

In the meantime, Daesh is simple, accurate and derogatory. That's why I use it.

---

[1] "The Irish Bataclan Hero," Sean Dunne, Irish Daily Mail. Dec. 21, 2015. http://www.dailymail.co.uk/news/article-3369806/The-story-modern-day-hero-Bataclan-massacre-survivor-tells-protected-girlfriend-gunmen-bullet-pulverised-foot-determination-learn-walk-wedding-day.html

[2] "Gunmen kill more than 120 in wave of attacks across Paris," Yahoo News. http://www.webcitation.org/6d1kwppjd

[3] "Paris attacks: who were the attackers?" BBC News, March 18, 2016. http://www.bbc.com/news/world-europe-34832512

[4] "Scene of Carnage Inside Sold-Out Paris Concert Hall," New York Times. Nov. 13, 2015. http://www.nytimes.com/2015/11/14/world/europe/paris-attacks.html?_r=0

---

[5] "Paris attacks: Terrorists played xylophone during Bataclan massacre," France 24. Dec. 29, 2015. http://www.france24.com/en/20151229-paris-attacks-investigation-bataclan-stadium-yanks-syria

[6] "Paris siege: Man posts live updates from inside Bataclan venue as hostages were shot "one by one," Independent UK. Nov. 14, 2015. http://www.independent.co.uk/news/world/europe/paris-siege-man-posts-live-updates-from-inside-bataclan-venue-as-hostages-were-shot-one-by-one-a6734486.html

[7] "Gunman yelled "For Iraq" — Ottawa shooting eyewitness," CBC News. Oct. 23, 2014. http://www.cbc.ca/news/canada/north/gunman-yelled-for-iraq-ottawa-shooting-eyewitness-1.2810689

[8] "6 honoured for helping Cpl. Nathan Cirillo during Parliament Hill shooting," CBC News. June 20, 2015. http://www.cbc.ca/news/canada/ottawa/6-honoured-for-helping-cpl-nathan-cirillo-during-parliament-hill-shootings-1.3121539

[9] *Ibid*

[10] "Michael Zehaf-Bibeau and Martin Couture-Rouleau: their shared traits," CBC News. Oct. 27, 2014. http://www.cbc.ca/news/canada/michael-zehaf-bibeau-and-martin-couture-rouleau-their-shared-traits-1.2812241

[11] Following the October 2014 terrorist attacks in Quebec and Ottawa, my husband and a few of his political friends started the Stand On Guard fund. Within a few days, the fund had raised hundreds of thousands dollars for the families of the two fallen soldiers. Even after their kickstarter campaign ended, the donations kept coming. They directed all funds to the True Patriot Love Foundation, a charity dedicated to helping the brave men and women who serve Canada.

[12] "Belgian Government admits it has lost control of No-Go Zones, Elliot Friedland. Clarion Project. Nov. 16, 2015. https://www.clarionproject.org/analysis/belgian-government-admits-it-has-lost-control-no-go-zone

[13] "Brussels can deploy all the troops it wants. It won't solve anything," , Haras Rafiq, Quilliam Foundation. March 24, 2016.

http://www.quilliamfoundation.org/blog/brussels-can-deploy-all-the-troops-it-wants-it-wont-solve-anything/

[14] "Belgium: A country of permanent migration," Milica Petrovic, Migration Policy Institute, Country Profile. Nov. 15, 2012. http://www.migrationpolicy.org/article/belgium-country-permanent-immigration

[15] "Free Movement Europe," Migration Policy Institute. http://www.migrationpolicy.org/article/free-movement-europe-past-and-present

[16] "Selection, Migration and Integration: Why Multiculturalism Works in Australia (and Fails in Europe)," Oliver Marc Hartwich, The Centre for Independent Studies. Policy Monographs. Sept. 1, 2011. https://www.cis.org.au/publications/policy-monographs/selection-migration-and-integration-why-multiculturalism-works-in-australia-and-fails-in-europe

[17] "Economic Impacts of Immigration: A Survey," Sari Pekkala Kerr and William R. Kerr, National Bureau of Economic Research. Harvard Business School, Jan. 2011. http://dl.kli.re.kr/dl_image/IMG/03/000000011124/SERVICE/000000011124_01.PDF

[18] "Belgium: A country of permanent migration," Milica Petrovic, Migration Policy Institute, Country Profile. Nov. 15, 2012. http://www.migrationpolicy.org/article/belgium-country-permanent-immigration

[19] "Selection, Migration and Integration: Why Multiculturalism Works in Australia (and Fails in Europe)," Oliver Marc Hartwich, The Centre for Independent Studies. Policy Monographs. Sept. 1, 2011. https://www.cis.org.au/publications/policy-monographs/selection-migration-and-integration-why-multiculturalism-works-in-australia-and-fails-in-europe

[20] "Muslim Americans: Middle Class and Mostly Mainstream," Pew Research Center. May 22, 2007. http://www.pewresearch.org/files/old-assets/pdf/muslim-americans.pdf

[21] "Selection, Migration and Integration: Why Multiculturalism Works in Australia (and Fails in Europe)," Oliver Marc Hartwich, The Centre for Independent Studies. Policy Monographs. Sept. 1, 2011.

https://www.cis.org.au/publications/policy-monographs/selection-migration-and-integration-why-multiculturalism-works-in-australia-and-fails-in-europe

[22] "Merkel says German multicultural society has failed," BBC News. Oct. 17, 2010. http://www.bbc.com/news/world-europe-11559451

[23] "Molenbeek broke my heart," Politico Europe. Nov. 21, 2015, Teun Voeten. http://www.politico.eu/article/molenbeek-broke-my-heart-radicalization-suburb-brussels-gentrification/

[24] "Who knows what horrors he has been through," Daily Mail. Jan. 27, 2016. http://www.dailymail.co.uk/news/article-3419094/Who-knows-horrors-Police-chief-sparks-anger-sympathising-Somali-boy-stabbed-refugee-worker.html

CHAPTER 2: IMPORTING THREATS TO CANADA

A Strange New World

The turning point in the 2015 Canadian election campaign came over the Labour Day long weekend, about halfway through the campaign, at a time when Justin Trudeau's Liberal Party was in third place and slightly trailing both the incumbent Conservatives and the New Democrats.

The election took a deciding twist when images surfaced of a lifeless toddler, three-year-old Alan Kurdi, lying dead on a beach in Turkey.

The boy, his brother, their mother and several others all drowned while trying to cross the Aegean Sea after fleeing the civil war in Syria. The heart-wrenching photo of young Alan came to represent the West's inaction and supposed indifference towards Syria; specifically, the refugee crisis and the plight of Syrians fleeing the ongoing civil war.

A sense of hysteria and guilt swept across Europe and made its way to Canada. As these haunting images circulated, Canadians from all backgrounds and political affiliations began to ask the government to do more.

To add to the frenzy, Canadian media erroneously reported that Alan's family had applied for refugee status in Canada and been rejected by the Harper government. This was untrue. It was the boy's uncle who had once submitted an incomplete application.

Regardless, the accusation added fuel to the fire of outrage, sadness, and guilt in Canada. The Kurdis had extended family in Canada, so it is likely that Canada was to be their final destination. And thus, the Harper government was blamed for its clumsy handling of the situation.

As a former drama teacher, and a man who made a small fortune giving speeches, Justin Trudeau's empathetic response was incredibly effective; his emotional reaction to the Syrian refugee crisis accurately mirrored the sentiments of Canadians in the moment.

"Canadians get it," said Trudeau. "This is about doing the right thing, about living up to the values that we cherish as a country."[1]

He went on to bash the Conservatives, saying "you don't get to suddenly discover compassion in the middle of an election campaign. You either have it or you don't."

Calls for drastically increased numbers of Syrian refugees began pouring in from influential Canadians across the country. The outcry was so loud that even retired Gen. Rick Hillier, Canada's former chief of defence staff — the highest ranked officer in the Canadian Forces — joined the chorus advocating for a massive influx of Syrians into Canada.

A hard-nosed man who once said his job was "to be able to kill people," even Gen. Hillier reacted with sympathy and urged the leaders of all three parties to "bring in 50,000 of those frightened men, women, and children to Canada" by the end of 2015.[2]

It was against this backdrop that Justin Trudeau made his bold humanitarian pledge to admit 25,000 Syrian refugees by the year's end.

Trudeau's refugee promise trumped those of both of the other parties — 21,000 over four years under the Conservatives and 15,000 in 2015 by the NDP — and helped lift his party to new levels of support.

The actual numbers didn't matter as much as the empathy shown by Trudeau, which stood in contrast to Harper's cold and aloof disposition.

In the October election, Trudeau won a sweeping majority government and his Syrian refugee pledge was a central component of his party's platform and election victory.

This context is incredibly important in the making of our refugee policy and certainly will have national security implications for years to come.

His campaign trail pledge was made while Trudeau was merely the leader of the third party. It was made on the fly, in between taking selfies, by a man without substantial knowledge of the various components and timelines involved with refugee resettlement. It was a Hail Mary pass; and one Justin Trudeau didn't expect anyone to catch.

When the Trudeau government was sworn into office, on November 4, 2015, the campaign promise collided with reality.

The government suddenly had mere weeks to expedite the process of assessing, screening, selecting and relocating tens of thousands of refugees from the midst of a war zone — a war zone that is a hotbed for radical Islamic terrorism.

In 2015, the standard timeline for Canadian immigration officials to process Syrian refugees was set at 13 months for government-assisted refugees and 27 months for privately-sponsored Syrian refugees.

Canada typically accepts about 25,000 total refugees per year —about 5,000 of those being government-sponsored refugees. All of a sudden the newly-elected prime minister had committed Canada to bringing in 25,000 government-sponsored refugees, all from Syria, in just under two months.

As Trudeau's new government was getting settled in and trying to figure out a plan for translating his promise into action, several global events rocked the western world and caused us all to stop for pause.

On November 13, just nine days after Trudeau had been sworn in as prime minister, Daesh terrorists carried out their coordinated terrorist attacks in Paris.

Nine terrorists killed 130 people, including 89 at the Bataclan Theatre, and injured 368 more — nearly 100 seriously. This was Daesh's first major attack against the West, and the deadliest raid on France since the

Second World War.

Even France's socialist president saw this for what it was, an act of war against France, and by extension — thanks to NATO's Article Five and the principle of collective defence — an attack on all western allies, including Canada.[3]

Daesh claimed responsibility for the civilian massacre, which was planned in Syria, organized in Belgium and perpetrated against the heart and soul of our western civilization, in Paris.

To add to the precariousness of the situation, French officials found that one of the Daesh attackers was carrying a Syrian passport,[4] confirming the suspicion held by many that radical Islamist militants had infiltrated the hordes of refugees flooding the continent.

It was later confirmed that two of the Paris massacre terrorists were EU nationals who left to fight alongside Daesh in the Middle East. These men were trained and groomed for the attack, then returned to Europe through the popular Eastern Mediterranean migrant route.

The men entered the EU through the Greek island of Leros and registered with authorities in Greece using fake Syrian passports. Untracked by authorities — the EU has no system for tracing the movement of migrants — these thugs made their way to Paris and were likely given government handouts and refugee benefits along the way.

A report by the EU's border safety agency did not mince words about the dangers of unscreened refugees.

"The Paris attacks in November 2015 clearly demonstrated that irregular migratory flows could be used by terrorists to enter the EU," the report concluded.[5]

A few weeks later, a husband-and-wife terrorist team carried out a massacre in San Bernardino, California. The couple, heavily armed with machine guns and improvised explosive devices (IEDs), dropped their infant child off with a grandparent and went to the husband's workplace, a government office.

There, they engaged in a violent killing spree. They murdered 14 people and seriously injured 22 more. The couple were later killed in a shootout with police.

Based on the stockpile of weapons in their car and at their home, it was easy to see that they had intended to carry out a much more significant attack. The man was an American-born Muslim, while his wife was a Pakistani native who had been radicalized in Saudi Arabia before coming to the U.S. to get married.

The wife had managed to pass Homeland Security screening and was given a Green Card despite an evidence trail of apparent radicalization. Both had pledged allegiance to Daesh and carried out their attack in the name of a religious war.

Back in Canada, the Trudeau government claimed these attacks would have no effect on its position on refugees. These unfathomable atrocities against civilians in the West, however, were playing heavily on the minds of most Canadians in the last weeks of 2015.

The attacks underscored the threat of jihadists infiltrating our immigration system. They provided a sobering reminder that terrorists thwarting our security barriers was not only plausible, it was probable.

Fortunately, the Trudeau government recognized that an artificial deadline, based on a political agenda, was both rash and unachievable. Canada's immigration and security officials were under enough pressure already; it was simply misguided for Trudeau to force these officials to work around the clock for no real reason, to meet his artificial year-end deadline. Especially considering that even the smallest error or lapse in judgment could have lethal consequences in Canada.

Unfortunately, rather than reconsidering its entire commitment to resettle 25,000 Syrian refugees, the government doubled down and merely gave itself a two-month extension. The new artificial deadline was pushed to February 29, 2016, and an embarrassed administration committed to welcoming another 10,000 to 25,000 Syrian refugees by the end of 2016.

It is important to identify the enemy we are fighting, and to correctly diagnose the enemy's motive. Here is a column I wrote on this very subject in the Toronto Sun following the terrifying string of Islamic terrorist attacks around the world.

Islamic terrorism is not our fault
January 16, 2016

A Canadian is among the dead in an Islamic terrorist attack on Thursday in the Indonesian capital of Jakarta. Daesh, also known as ISIS or the Islamic State, has taken responsibility, marking their second deadly foreign attack this week. Just two days earlier, a suicide bomber targeted tourists outside Istanbul's famous Blue Mosque.

The Jakarta attacks were described by those on the ground as a "Paris-style massacre," with explosions and gunfire simultaneously rocking the Southeast Asian city. What a sad reminder of our time — that Paris, once known as the City of Light and Europe's cultural capital, has now become synonymous with mass murder and senseless attacks against civilians going about their daily lives.

These attacks show a departure in strategy by the so-called Islamic State. Daesh was once only concerned with a ground war in Iraq and Syria, and building their 'caliphate,' or Islamic kingdom governed by fundamentalist Sunni teachings. But they are now launching more and more attacks outside the Middle East.

The assaults against Istanbul and Jakarta also contradict a common narrative — that Daesh's terrorist attacks are mere retaliation for western sins.

A popular opinion on the political left is that Islamic State terrorists only attack those who stand in their way. Those who don't participate in the coalition bombing campaign, such as Costa Rica and Sweden, some argue, do not get attacked.

A Russian airliner was brought down over Sinai last year because of Putin's involvement in Iraq and Syria. Paris was attacked because of France's role in the coalition airstrikes.

And the San Bernardino attack was a result of America's long involvement in Middle Eastern affairs.

Some Canadians are susceptible to this narrative. A recent poll found that 10 per cent of Canadians who oppose our involvement in the bombing mission cite “fear of backlash” as the reason.

If we interfere in Daesh’s rampage over there, the thinking goes, they will come over here and attack us.

The problem with this line of thinking is that it seeks to rationalize, and even justify, the acts of radicals and extremists. It also simply doesn’t stand up to the facts.

Islamic terrorism is not a grievance-based conflict. It is not driven by inequality or exclusion. Like the 9/11 hijackers, Daesh terrorists typically come from middle class backgrounds and educated families.

These radical Islamists are fighting an ideological war. They kill innocent victims because they want to overthrow our society and impose their radical Islamic values onto others. They want us all living under their Sharia.

Turkey and Indonesia — both considered among the most secular and moderate of the world’s Muslim countries — have not provoked Daesh.

The opposite is true. Russia recently accused Turkey of being a secret terrorist ally and propping up Daesh by buying their oil.

Indonesia, the world’s most populous Muslim country, has not offered military support or joined the U.S.-led bombing coalition in Iraq and Syria. Instead, they’ve focused on fostering peace and tolerance at home, and avoided getting drawn into the conflicts of the Middle East.

Neither is standing in Daesh’s way. But just like France and the United States, these countries are still targeted.

Islamic terrorists are provoking a global war against non-believers, including against moderate Muslims. If you reject and refuse to cower to their archaic and oppressive laws, you are their enemy.

The sooner we come to terms with these truths, and stop pretending this is all our fault, the better equipped we will be to fight and win this war.

Winning Hearts (Not Minds)

Justin Trudeau's humanitarian impulses make him a hero among the world's progressive elites. It makes us feel good to help others, and Trudeau has mastered the art of feel-good politics.

In a campaign to win over the hearts and minds of Canadians, Trudeau managed to win over our hearts with his compassion, at the expense of our minds.

Despite his having the unanimous endorsement of adoring elites, many thinking Canadians have yet to endorse Trudeau's refugee policy. That's because Trudeau has failed to acknowledge any of the valid safety concerns and security implications.

When it comes to our safety and security, Trudeau and his team seem to have other priorities: Justin Trudeau would rather go to a photoshoot at the airport with newly arriving Syrians than have a serious discussion about national security.

The Trudeau Liberals refuse to deal with these threats responsibly, because doing so would be counter to their political objectives.

Acknowledging a national security threat would be an implicit acceptance of all the risks to Canada that come along with Trudeau's decision to rush in tens of thousands of refugees without proper planning, without thorough security checks and without planning for their integration into our society.

Besides, Trudeau's vacuous philosophy of "sunny ways" does not lend itself to such deep and serious thinking and planning.

Trudeau's approach to politics — style over substance — does not easily align with a serious risk assessment of counter-terrorism, asymmetrical warfare, and migration policy in the 21st century.

This is the man, after all, who said Stephen Harper only joined the U.S.-led bombing coalition against Daesh because he wanted to "whip out our CF-18s to show them how big they are."

This is the man who once suggested that Vladimir Putin annexed Crimea, after invading Ukraine — a sovereign state — because Putin was mad the Russian men's hockey team lost at the 2014 Sochi Olympics.

This is the man who, in the aftermath of the Boston Marathon bombing, reminded his CBC audience of the importance of reflecting on the "root causes" of terrorism.

Just read, word for word, what Justin Trudeau said in response to the simple question, after the Boston terrorist attacks, "what would you do?" if he were the Canadian prime minister.

> "First thing, um, you offer support and sympathy and condolences and, you know, can we send down, you know, EMTs (emergency medical teams) or, I mean, as we contributed after 9/11? I mean, is there any material immediate support we have, we can offer?
>
> And then at the same time, you know, over the coming days, we have to look at the root causes. Now we don't know now whether it was, you know, terrorism or a single crazy or, you know, a domestic issue or a foreign issue, I mean, all of those questions.
>
> But there is no question that this happened because there is someone who feels completely excluded, completely at war with innocents, at war with a society. And our approach has to be, okay, where do those tensions come from?
>
> I mean, yes, we need to make sure that we're promoting security and we're, you know, keeping our borders safe and, you know, monitoring the kinds of, you know, violent subgroups that happen around.
>
> But we also have to monitor and encourage people to not point fingers at each other and lay blame for personal ills or societal ills on a specific group, whether it be the West or the government or Bostonians or whatever it is, because it's that idea of dividing humans against ourselves, of pointing out that they're not like us and, you know, in order to achieve our political goals, we can kill innocents here. That is something that no society in the world that is healthy, regardless of ideology, will accept. And yet, it is something that is happening increasingly across this world."

This is the raw, unedited Justin Trudeau. And this is how he actually thinks and talks … that is, when he isn't repeating canned lines or reading from a teleprompter.

In the wake of a deadly terrorist attack on a major U.S. city, Justin Trudeau diverged into a rambling, incoherent, high school-level diatribe about tolerance and trying to understand terrorists.

Sure, Trudeau admits we should, you know, promote security and, you know, keep our borders safe, and stuff … but he fails to mention the victims, their families or the immense suffering these terrorists inflicted upon innocent civilians.

And of course, he doesn't address how a radical Islamist ideology drives these terrorists.

Trudeau can barely muster the courage to condemn this violence, instead criticizing those "dividing humans against ourselves" — blaming both radical Islamists and western democracies at the same time.

If Trudeau had been Canada's prime minister back then, his top priority would not be to find and stop the enemy, but instead to rationalize violence and think about the root causes. Rather than ordering the police and the security forces to track down terrorists, Trudeau would have wanted us to meditate about the ways we were at fault and the ways that western society was to blame for those who feel "completely excluded."

With this track record, should we really be surprised that now-Prime Minister Trudeau wants to throw our doors open to the masses of migrants streaming out of the Middle East?

Without any real concern that some of these migrants may be radicalized terrorists?

Trudeau thinks that so long as he's in charge — as long as he's there at the airport to offer a big hug to all newcomers — that the terrorists will put down their weapons, become law-abiding Canadians, discover a new appreciation for freedom and democracy and, of course, join the Liberal Party of Canada.

Trudeau doesn't take the threat of radical Islamic terrorism seriously, because he seriously thinks that his Liberal multiculturalism is the antidote to violent jihad.

IMMEDIATE SECURITY THREATS

In the real world, there are serious challenges that limit the Canadian government's ability to properly vet and screen Syrian refugees.

The U.S. Senate committee on Homeland Security conducted hearings in January 2016, and heard testimony from leading Canadian and American national security scholars and officials on Trudeau's expedited refugee settlement plan and its implications for U.S. national security.

While Canada's Immigration Minister John McCallum brushed off the hearing as "a Tea Party operation,"[6] the bi-partisan committee openly discussed their concerns with Trudeau's capacity to keep our shared continent safe.

Analysts on both sides of the border are demanding proof, not just assurances, that the Trudeau government is not taking shortcuts or sacrificing security to achieve its political objectives.

McCallum thinks that by dismissing our American allies and neighbours as a bunch of right-wing fear-mongers that he can shrug off the unavoidable risks associated with resettling refugees from a war zone, in the middle of an active war.

The inconvenient truth is that Canada has never had the ability, and does not have the ability today, to properly screen and vet 25,000 Syrians in just four months, much less screen another 25,000 refugees in the 10 months to follow.

FBI director James Comely said that U.S. intelligence services would have trouble screening 10,000 Syrians in one year.

Meanwhile, despite being one-tenth the size of the United States — and without the resources of the FBI, CIA, NSA, U.S. Army Intelligence, or the Department of Homeland Security — Canada is forging ahead with a plan to admit five times that many refugees in just 14 months.

Trudeau's sunny optimism aside, it is impossible for the government to ensure, on that timetable, that no jihadist agents will enter Canada, disguised as refugees.

This isn't just a stab in the dark. Daesh itself has boasted, repeatedly, that it is sending its militants into the West amidst the chaos and confusion of the refugee crisis.

With millions of people flooding out of the Middle East, Daesh has given interviews and explained its strategy of planting agents in with the flow of refugees. "Just wait," said a Daesh militant to a BuzzFeed reporter in early 2015. They are working with smugglers to embed fighters into the tide of refugees. "They are going like refugees," he said, "we will send them on the next ship."[7]

Plain-clothed terrorists, after all, look strikingly similar to bona fide Syrian refugees. Rob Wainwright, chief of the European Union's police agency Europol, recently confirmed these fears by stating his agency knows of at least 5,000 Daesh jihadists who have snuck into Europe using the refugee route. This is the terrifying consequence of Europe's mindless approach to refugee policy.

Europe's leaders, through an open border policy and a hands-off approach to integration, have put their their own citizens on the front line of a hot war.

Under Stephen Harper, and successive immigration ministers Jason Kenney and Chris Alexander, Canada took a more cautious approach.[8]

But just because we have historically had a better security apparatus and integration strategy than Europe, it does not make us immune to jihadi violence. The same tactics can and do apply to refugees coming to North America.

Consider that Canada accepts refugees through the United Nation High Commission on Refugees (UNHCR). We select refugees from the UNHCR camps and communities in Lebanon, Jordan and Turkey.

Lebanese cabinet minister Elias Bou Saab has warned that Daesh has infiltrated UNHCR camps in Lebanon.[9] He suggests that approximately two per cent of the 1.1 million Syrian refugees camped in Lebanon have connections to Daesh. That means that upwards of 20,000 UNHCR refugees may be Islamic State jihadists in disguise.

There are terrorists amid the refugees; even refugees who have been pre-approved by the United Nations and hand-picked for resettlement. This fact is undeniable. That we want to help ease the suffering around the world does not change this fact. And as conservative journalist Ben Shapiro likes to say, the facts don't care about our feelings.

Likewise, public opinion polling indicates that up to 20 per cent of the Syrian population believes that Daesh has a positive influence in their country[10]. Furthermore, according to the Arab Center for Research and Policy Studies, 13 per cent of Syrians in refugee camps in Lebanon, Jordan and Turkey have a positive opinion of Daesh.[11]

It turns out that some Syrians like extreme terrorist groups. Even refugees are products of their upbringing and of their society; in this case, a society ripe with ethnic hatreds, sectarian violence and centuries of a cruel and barbaric tribal warfare.

One in five Syrians directly supports Daesh. Presumably, many more have positive perceptions of other terrorist groups.

Many likely agree with radical elements of Daesh's religion and ideology. There is a reason that Syria is caught up in a long and bloody civil war; Syria's civil society is marred with ancient blood feuds and intolerance toward others. Many possess an ideology that is incompatible with the West.

Just because one side in the conflict is being murdered and chased away doesn't make them liberal-minded. In the case of Syria, the refugees are coming from the same villages, the same madrassas and sometimes the same families as the terrorists.

Coming from the same family as a terrorist obviously does not make you guilty by association. It does, however, require that Canadian officials be extremely vigilant in screening and vetting your application to come to Canada.

Herein lies the reality of the struggle of asymmetrical warfare. The enemy is no longer easily recognizable. Wars are no longer declared, fought, won or lost and ended with formal surrenders. There are no longer presentations of swords, negotiations of reparations and treaties or ends of war marked with dancing and celebrations.

In the 21st century, wars are ongoing, our enemies live among us and civilians are drafted to the front lines. Innocent people, unarmed women and children, are targeted first and foremost. They are the softest targets.

Many Canadians will point to our long and proud history of resettling refugees — loyalists coming up from the United States after their revolutionary war, 250,000 Europeans following the Second World War, the Vietnamese boat people in the early 1980s and so on — to show that Canada has always welcomed newcomers with open arms.

This is absolutely true, with one major distinction.

Canada historically has opened its doors <u>after</u> a war has ended. The war against Daesh and radical Islam is still being fought.

Most Canadians believe that something must be done to assist the Syrian refugees — that we should not wait until the war is over to offer our help.

But the way the Trudeau government is selecting refugees from Syria to resettle into Canada should raise some eyebrows.

Canada's refugee policy does not seek to help those most at risk in Syria. Rather, we select the refugees at the front of a queue organized by a very flawed agency — the United Nations High Commission on Refugees.

The vast majority of Syrian refugees registering with the UNHCR and pouring into refugee camps are Sunni Muslims who are being targeted by Syrian President Bashar al-Assad — a Shi'ite Muslim from the Ba'ath Party. Daesh, built out of the rubble of this civil war in Syria, attracts the most radical members of this Sunni population.

Most Sunni Muslims are not terrorists. The majority reject Daesh and its violence. But some do have links to Daesh. Others believe in the same fundamentalist doctrine of Islam.

These Sunni Muslims dominate the UNHCR camps and are often hostile to outsiders.

Meanwhile, Daesh is committing genocide against the Yazidi people — an ancient Kurdish tribe with mixed Christian beliefs — as well as Assyrian Christians and other ethnic minorities in the region.

Daesh is intentionally targeting and slaughtering ethnic minorities, and forcing these ancient Christian communities to desperately flee for safety. In the Sunni-dominated UNHCR camps, these persecuted minorities have little support and nowhere to go.

First-hand accounts of the situation in Syria tell us that Christian refugees avoid the UN camps out of fear of intimidation: discrimination from local Syrian UN employees and abuse from other refugees.

In fact, most Christians in Iraq and Syria do not even bother registering with the UN. Of course, the UN denies any wrongdoing, but the numbers show a different story.

Of the millions of Syrian refugees registered with UNHCR camps in neighbouring Egypt, Jordan, Lebanon and Iraq, only 1 per cent are Christians.

In 2015, Christians made up more than 10 per cent of Syria's population. In a typical war zone, you would expect refugee camps to be disproportionately filled with persecuted ethnic and religious minorities. Not the other way around.

Christian Solidarity Worldwide, a British non-profit organization that works with Syrian refugees, publicly spoke out against the UN, saying that local Syrian Christians are scared by "the strict Muslim environment dominating the camps."[12]

Under the UN's watch, Christians are being bullied for not wearing Muslim clothing, harassed for the way they pray, pressured by those trying to convert them and intimidated by those forcing them to abide by a strict interpretation of Islam.

The UN is failing to secure its camps and keep refugees safe. And yet, Canada's official refugee resettlement policy is to only select refugees referred by the UNHCR

We know that Daesh is committing genocide against Christian communities in the Middle East. Both the UN and the U.S. Secretary of State John Kerry have conceded this sad reality. Yet Trudeau's focus remains on helping only those who have registered with the United Nations.

Rather than helping the most in need, rather than sponsor the refugees we know are not members of Daesh — the persecuted minorities such as the Yazidis and Assyrians — Trudeau's policy focuses squarely on resettling refugees chosen from amongst the same Sunni community whose more militant members are terrorizing Christians in the region.

Under the Harper government, and particularly thanks to the efforts of Jason Kenney, Canada developed a policy to seek out the most at-risk and threatened religious minorities for resettlement into Canada. We made a concerted effort to provide assistance to the most vulnerable people and bring the most persecuted minorities to safety in Canada. But everything changed when Trudeau was elected.

Trudeau has said outright, on the 2015 election campaign trail, that he does not agree with sponsoring persecuted ethnic and religious minority groups to be refugees in Canada.

When asked by a reporter if he would continue the policy of prioritizing persecuted ethnic and religious minorities from Iraq and Syria, he responded by accusing Harper of picking and choosing refugee applicants for political purposes. Trudeau said the idea of the Prime Minister's Office selecting refugees was "disgusting."[13]

When asked again if he would prioritize religious minorities through Canada's refugee program, Trudeau was abundantly clear. "Ab-so-lute-ly not," he said with a smirk.

Why would we? Trudeau's approach to refugee policy is not about helping those most in need. It is not about alleviating the suffering of the most abused and most persecuted in the region. No. Canada's refugee policy is based on showing the world that Canada cares.

Trudeau's decision to accept 50,000 refugees is an exercise in "virtue signaling," to borrow an expression from a security expert and recent co-panelist at a conference at which I spoke in Washington, D.C.[14] It's an applause line in a speech, a bragging right for Trudeau to use while doing television interviews and speaking at conferences abroad.

The policy has more to do with Trudeau himself than the people it purports to help. Trudeau's refugee pledge is designed to show the world that he is not concerned with radical Islamists. It's a demonstration by the Trudeau government that Islamist and jihadist violence are not a real threat to Canada.

This is the application of Trudeau's "root causes" pop psychology. As long as Canada is super nice to all Muslims, including extreme Islamist groups, we will be safe from their terrorism. Trudeau is simply proving a point. And he doesn't care if the rest of us pay the price.

The Syrian Theatre

In addition to the direct warnings from Daesh agents, and the empirical evidence of terrorists-posing-as-refugees, there are also enormous unknowns due to the collapse of the Syrian state.

Syria has, since 2011, been submerged in a bloody civil war. What were at first moderate Arab Spring protests turned violent when the regime of dictator Bashar al-Assad used force against protestors, engaging in mass arrests and killings.

As other Arab Spring protests failed or succeeded around the Middle East, dictated largely by the reaction and intervention of the West, mobs of militants and radicals streamed into Syria to back the anti-government rebels. Quickly, the conflict escalated into full-fledged civil war. As fighting intensified, U.S. President Barack Obama clumsily drew a red line, stating that the movement of chemical weapons would change the equation and prompt U.S. intervention.

Months later, when it was proven beyond any doubt that Assad was using chemical weapons against his own citizens, Obama was called on his bluff and failed to launch military action.

Obama's hesitation and inaction changed the war in Syria. It emboldened the world's rogue actors.

Radical elements of the anti-Assad militias split and joined an al-Qaeda affiliate in Iraq, declaring a new Islamic kingdom and an end to the Sykes-Picot line — the border that had divided Syria and Iraq since the French and British carved up the territory following the collapse of the Ottoman Empire and the First World War.

These terrorist militants, including former members of Saddam Hussein's regime, announced the creation of a Caliphate, or Islamic kingdom governed by strict Sharia, and began their horrific crusade against any and all who stood in their way.

These militants were armed with the most advanced and sophisticated military equipment in the world: stolen arms American left behind from the 2003 Iraq war.[15]

Daesh is the first terrorist group to wage war on a digital front, the first to use a sophisticated social media campaign to recruit foreign fighters into their fold and broadcast their atrocities to the world.

Traditional wars were fought on land, sea, air and space; Daesh has opened the cyber propaganda front as the fifth domain of warfare.

Making Obama's "red line" blunder worse, his administration refused to take the threat of Daesh seriously. As the terrorists were confiscating American weapons, stealing Iraq's oil, capturing large swaths of territory, terrorizing all who stood in their path and positioning for genocide against the Yazidis, Obama flippantly referred to them as al-Qaeda's junior-varsity team.

Like Trudeau, Obama wanted to paint a rosy picture of the world, and stand by his election pledge to withdraw American troops from Iraq, regardless of the power vacuum it created. America stood by as Daesh gained strength, redefined digital warfare and committed genocide.

While Obama's ineptitude contributed to the rise of Daesh in Iraq, it is wrong to level blame on the United States for the broader mess in Syria.

Syria's oppressive and heavy-handed Assad regime has very little to do with America; the U.S. has had little to do with Syria since its inception as a state in 1919. If you want to blame an outside power for Assad rule, blame France or Russia or Iran.

The Americans have little history in Syria. But the U.S. is culpable for retreating from the Middle East at the worst possible time for Syria's stability. Obama envisioned a post-American Middle East, without really knowing what that would look like. We know now: it looks like Syria in 2016.

The Syrian civil war can best be described as a proxy war. In the Syrian war theatre, we are seeing both the existential crisis tearing at Islam and pitting Sunnis against Shi'ites, and a proxy of a post-American-led world order, where regional and global wannabe-superpowers flex their might, waging stand-in battles.

The Shi'ite Assad regime is supported by Iran and its affiliates — Qods Force and Hezbollah — as well as Russia. The Sunni rebels are supported by Saudi Arabia, while the U.S.-led coalition is supporting the Kurds, who are also fighting for an independent Kurdistan, a territory covering parts of Iraq, Iran and Turkey.

While the Sunni-led Daesh has succeed in galvanizing the world against it — with its propaganda, torture videos and genocide — they are fighting against the Kurds, the Assad regime and other rebel groups, including moderate Sunnis.

Turkey, a NATO member and longtime ally of the West, has positioned itself precariously in this conflict — buying oil reserves from Daesh and thereby funding its entire operation — and directly attacking the Kurds in Northern Iraq. Turkey has also engaged in acts of provocation against Russia, shooting down Russian jets for allegedly entering Turkish airspace.

Amidst the chaos, the Assad regime has lost control over its governing institutions. It has become a failed state. This makes it nearly impossible for the UNHCR to request information and records on citizens and refugees. UN officials cannot reliably verify a refugee applicant's identity; Canadian security and immigration officers cannot reliably perform a criminal record check on a refugee claimant with local officials. There are no local officials, and therefore, there are no background checks.

Combined with the inability to perform background checks, is a thriving black market for fake and stolen Syrian passports. International media have documented that rebel groups and militias have taken over passport facilities across Syria and Iraq. This means that Daesh, and others, now have the capacity to print official Syrian passports and travel documents. Even the real passports are fake.

Since Europe primarily accepts and gives preferential treatment to Syrians, there is a thriving market for Syrian passports, which are readily available to fraudsters, criminals and terrorists throughout the Middle East.

An analysis by German officials found that eight per cent of Syrian passports used in Germany were fake. Considering that Germany does not regularly check passports at points of entry, that number is likely a conservative estimate.

The prevalence of fake or stolen passports throws the entire verification process into question. It is plausible that many refugees living in UNHCR camps have lied or misrepresented themselves in order to gain entry to the camps, and are now patiently waiting to be resettled into the West — sleeper agents living amongst the refugees selected for relocation into Canada.

Fraud and the Fallout

There are 4.2 million Syrian refugees registered with the UNHCR, and Canada was only looking to find 25,000 for resettlement into Canada. Pretty good odds of landing the most attractive newcomers, right?

That means Canada could reject 167 out of every 168 applicants, or select only the 99th percentile applicants. Or does it?

Thanks to Trudeau's rash political timeline, those odds were tossed on their head. A report found that 95 per cent of Syrian refugees contacted by the UNHCR turned Canada down and rejected the invitation for relocation.[16] They'd rather live in squalor in UN camps and wait out the war than move to the Great White North.

This embarrassing revelation put Canada into a troubling situation. It made us vulnerable and even desperate to select from a narrowed pool of applicants. Beggars can't be choosers. And since the overwhelming majority of bona fide Syrian refugees weren't exactly jumping up and down and asking for resettlement to Canada, it is reasonable to ask whether the small minority of those willing to come might include some with murderous intentions.

Canada's security and immigration establishment was already trying to cope with conditions in the war zone, making it difficult, if not impossible, to verify and scrutinize identities and backgrounds of would-be migrants.

The new political element made the job that much more challenging. The Trudeau government tacitly acknowledged the threat of terrorists infiltrating the system, when it decided to limit refugee applications only to women and families with children, announcing explicitly it would not accept single males.[17]

The Trudeau government considers Syrian women to be a "low risk group." Sixty per cent of Syrian refugees to date have been adult women, and 22 per cent are children.[18]

But how realistic is it to categorize half the Syrian population as "a low-risk group?"

Daesh has become a well-known destination for so-called jihadist brides, including high-profile cases such as the three British teenage girls who left London, traveled through Istanbul into Syria and handed themselves over the Islamic State.

These girls were born in Britain, raised in middle-class homes in North London and were the children of Muslim migrants. The girls' parents had left the Middle East to flee violence and war; to spare their families from the kind of horror that their daughters readily embraced.

The story of these London girls mirrors the story of a teenage girl in Birmingham, Alabama, who lied to her parents about a school trip to Atlanta, then hopped on a plane to Turkey and made her way into Syria.

Strikingly similar cases continue to emerge, of teenage girls and young women choosing to leave behind the comforts of the western world to engage in tribal warfare in Iraq and Syria.

The New York Times profiled two teenage girls living in Raqqa who are part of the Khansaa Brigade, an all-female "moral police force" within Daesh. Women play a dominant role in the new terrorist society, both as brides, morality police and even militants.

Limiting our Syrian refugees to women and families may sound good enough for Trudeau, but it is a risky and unproven security measure.

Being part of a family does not preclude someone from being radicalized or engaging in jihadi violence. Just look at the San Bernardino attackers, who were the parents of a young child.

The attackers dropped their young baby off with a family member on the way to carrying out their massacre. Many of the suicide bombers and Daesh agents have wives and children.

And again with a lack of verification, there is no certainty that the family with whom someone is travelling or living is actually their family. If someone shows up with an infant, the UNHCR agents have no way to know whether they are a bona fide family or if their story is a lie.

So the Trudeau government's assurance that it rejects "unaccompanied" men, instead prioritizing women, children and families, is still problematic. While it may help narrow the pool of potential refugees and somewhat streamline the selection process, it does not eliminate the risk of a terrorist entering Canada.

While it is easy to be critical of Trudeau's foolhardy Syrian refugee policy, we should take some solace in the integrity of our system and in the integrity of Canada's uncompromising security and immigration officials. They are second to none when it comes to their professionalism, procedures and diligence.

Unlike Europe, Canada is individually selecting its refugees. Canadian security officials exercise heightened scrutiny. They have a zero-tolerance policy: if a Canadian security official has any doubt whatsoever about an applicant throughout the screening process, that person's file is "put aside."

That's Canadian for saying they are rejected.

Furthermore, the information sharing and security cooperation agreements between Canada and the U.S. — covering security, border crossings, law enforcement and intelligence — are the most comprehensive of their kind between two nations.

Canadian officials check all biometric and biological data against U.S. criminal, immigration and security databases. This, again, highlights a major difference between North America and Europe, who struggles to share information across nation-states despite its union.

Canada's level of attention and scrutiny is no less thorough than that of our American counterparts. Canada uses the same security techniques and protocols as our neighbours, and we practice the same, or higher, level of vigilance.

The screening process is long and thorough. Applicants are first vetted by the UNHCR and then referred to Canadian immigration officials, who determine whether the candidates meet our refugee criteria and admissibility laws.

If a case meets our standards, the person is invited for an interview with a Canadian official. Following this interview — a key step that goes beyond the normal screening of potential migrants — the applicant is required to undergo full health examinations and further security screening.

From my experiences working in the Canadian government, for the Department of Citizenship and Immigration Canada, and from reading hundreds of deportation orders and case files where a person was deemed "inadmissible" to Canada, I can certainly attest that Canadian security officials are not bleeding-heart liberals like their current political overlords.

These are hard-nosed, level-headed, no-nonsense professionals. They put the safety and security of Canadians above all else.

I am thankful for their tough attitude and commitment to our national security and the integrity of our immigration system.

Consider one case where officials put Canadian security ahead ahead of compassion for a refugee applicant with terrorist associations. The case involved a gay Palestinian Christian convert who fled the West Bank to come to Canada as a teenager. Canadian officials deemed that he was inadmissible because he had been trained as a child to become an agent in the terrorist group Hamas.

The boy's family was Hamas royalty; his grandfather helped found the group and his uncles were all active terrorists in Israel.

Despite his grooming, however, the boy rejected his family's wishes, ran away from home and eventually moved to Canada where he asked for asylum. But Canada's immigration officials said no. They rejected his refugee application and tried to deport this young man because of his prior training, terrorist affiliations and inconsistencies in his story over the years. They put Canada's national security ahead of everything else.

I believed the young man should be permitted asylum. When CNN reported the story, it contacted his radical Palestinian parents, who threatened to kill their son if he ever returned.[19] Canada has a policy that it does not deport someone to an unsafe place where their life would be threatened, and thus, after a long ordeal, the young man was permitted to stay in Canada.

Selection and Integration

Our security officials do the best work they can under the circumstances, but they are limited in their capacity. Aside from the risk that Daesh terrorists will thwart our immigration system, infiltrate Canada and carry out a deadly attack, there is an equally menacing threat that comes alongside mass migration from Syria and the Middle East.

Just as some migrants may try to bring their war with them, others carry tribal feuds, ancient hatreds and deep illiberalism to their new home.

This is an ever-present but rarely mentioned threat that comes from resettling populations from regions prone to conflict and war. The risk of Canada's refugee resettlement program may persist long after the crisis in Syria fades away.

In just 14 months, Canada will have resettled up to 50,000 Syrian refugees. To use the Lebanese cabinet minister's math, if two per cent of these refugees are Daesh agents, that could mean that 1,000 terrorists will have managed to sneak into Canada. But to use the British public opinion data from the summer of 2015, if 20 per cent of Syria's population supports Daesh, that also means that 10,000 of the 50,000 refugees may be radicalized or possess a hateful and intolerant worldview.

A good migration policy has two fundamental pillars: first, you select the best people for resettlement. Then, you properly welcome and integrate these people into your society.

Both components are equally important — selection and integration. So far, Trudeau is getting them both wrong.

When it comes to selection, even if Canada's immigration and security officials could guarantee with certainty that no terrorist will enter Canada disguised as a Syrian refugee, they can't guarantee the refugees do not possess an illiberal and hateful worldview.

Our immigration officials interview potential refugees — through a translator — but they do not ask questions about a person's ideology or worldview. A few basic questions about living in a western pluralist society would go a long way toward stopping a potential tide of intolerance from flowing into Canada.

Here are five basic questions that should be asked of all newcomers, before they are accepted and admitted into Canada:

1. Do you think men and women should have equal rights?
2. Do you believe in religious freedom for everyone?
3. Gay marriage is legal in Canada. Are you okay with that?
4. Your neighbour may be African or Chinese. Are you okay with that? Your child may go to school, sit together and play with a Jewish child. Are you okay with that?
5. Will you uphold Canada's laws and respect Canadian values?

Sure, a newcomers may lie about their beliefs in order to gain entry into Canada, but at least they will know what to expect when they arrive here.

Canadian pluralism should be presented to newcomers before they are invited to migrate here. If newcomers cannot or will not accept our values, they should not be allowed to board their flight to Pearson International.

Canadians are fortunate that, as a society, we have developed a peaceful and pluralistic culture. We have, by and large, pushed bigotry and hatred into the dark, marginal caves and recesses of our society where few dare to venture. It would be a great shame to start importing these views via mass migration.

The Nobel laureate Milton Friedman taught that open border policies are incompatible with the welfare state. If a nation offers a rich smorgasbord of government handouts to all citizens, and also allows open borders, people from all over the world will arrive to take advantage without contributing to the host society, its economy or its public finances.

To combat the free-rider problem, a welfare-state society would soon be forced to to draw borders around its benefits and handouts, and create distinctions and various classes of citizenship — which is precisely what Liberal politicians like Justin Trudeau claim to stand against.

But this is what we see in Europe, where open-border policies have led to several generations of migrants living in Switzerland, Sweden and Germany, without ever receiving citizenship. Second-class citizenship for immigrants in these nations is a fact of life.

Friedman's concept of the incompatibility of open borders with the welfare state can also be applied to other aspects of our society: this is true of democracy too.

We are only as strong as our population is educated. If we throw open our doors to hateful and intolerant people, in a generation or two, Canada will regress into a backward country.

A transformed populace could vote away our freedoms and elect tyrants like those who rule the lands these refugees have fled. If we import the bitter attitudes and tribal feuds that led to civil war in Syria, we may well eventually import their war as well.

That is why we must select peace-loving people who want to leave war behind. People who embrace Canada's culture and values.

This doesn't mean we should exclude Muslims. It does, however, mean that we must exclude *some* Muslims.

At the height of the troubles in Northern Ireland, the leading actors in the conflict were all observant Christians, with heightened loyalties to their particular denomination that made Christians in other parts of the world, even in England, shake their heads.

Northern Irish immigrants to Canada no longer get the type of scrutiny their applications did in the 1960s and 1970s for connections to sectarian groups notionally affiliated to Christianity. That's because many years have passed since these groups have been associated with bloodshed on a massive scale.

Just as those with ties to violent Northern Irish groups received additional scrutiny back then, so too should individuals with ties to violent Islamist groups receive additional scrutiny today.

Which leads to the second pillar of a good migration system. Integration is in many ways the more challenging aspect of a good migration policy. Integration requires a long-term commitment by our political leaders as well as civil society to engage with newcomers and make them feel welcome.

That's why Canada's integration policies, and the work of our resettlement agencies and organizations, is just as important as the work done by our security and immigration officials. When newcomers arrive in Canada, especially those who may be prone to radicalized ideologies, we must extend to them a proper welcome and invite them to actively integrate into Canadian society.

We need to engage them directly. We need to encourage them, repeatedly, to participate in Canadian life.

This is the important role that civil society, not solely government, must play in resettling refugees. Churches, charities, businesses, families and individuals do most of the heavy lifting when it comes to engaging and welcoming newcomers.

Indeed, with the recent wave of Syrian refugees, it's everyday Canadians who have taken over where the Trudeau government has failed.

Whether it is the volunteers who lead clothing and food drives for newcomers, members of the Vancouver Canucks who took a day to give Syrian newcomers a tour of the city, or the Glen Bernard summer camp in Ontario which is offering free spots for Syrian girls, everyday Canadians are stepping up and helping wherever they can.

Meanwhile, when it comes to government-led refugee integration, Trudeau's approach is proving just as reckless as his selection process.

As Trudeau was being feted in elite international circles for his "generosity," resettlement workers and agencies — the people who work on the ground with refugees — were completely overwhelmed. Particularly the government-funded groups who work with refugees coming to Canada through the government-led program. In cities across Canada, these agencies asked the Trudeau government for a "pause" in accepting newcomers.

"A pause." That is the Canadian way of saying that the Trudeau government's approach was turning into a slow-motion train wreck.

"The timing just needs to be spread out a bit, it's just been this huge influx," said Leslie Emory, director of the Ottawa Immigrant Community Services Organization.[20] She was not alone. In the span of just a few days, resettlement agencies in Toronto, Vancouver, Halifax, Calgary and Ottawa all asked the government to slow down or halt the number of refugees being sent to their cities.

In the rush to get so many Syrians into Canada, the Liberals never bothered consulting with the people who work with refugees once they arrive. These agencies and networks are responsible for ensuring that newcomers can actually live their lives in Canada, meeting such basic needs as housing, food, medical care, proper clothing, banking, English or French classes, schools and child care for the children. And they were completely overwhelmed.

These groups were so overburdened, and so desperate, they had to speak out to the media. They had to ring the alarm bell because Trudeau's policies risk creating serious and long-term integration problems.

These agencies play a vital role in ensuring refugees and ensuring they are content and connected to the broader community.

Reports of Syrian refugees being ignored and neglected — many spending their first months in Canada crammed with their children into budget motels, getting no information from the Trudeau government — do not bode well for our future. This isolation, this first impression, can sow the seeds of discontentment with Canada and Canadians.

Welcoming refugees is difficult work. It is a long and ongoing struggle. Accommodating newcomers from a bloody and traumatic civil war carries a new set of problems for both the host society and refugees.

That is why, when discussing the number of refugees Canada will accept in any given year, it's necessary to look at the big picture of resettlement, well beyond the airport photo shoot.

Without the proper support networks, without persistent, active engagement with a broader community of Canadians, without deliberate cultural education, we run the risk of forcing refugees into their own isolated societies.

Without significant incentives and encouragement, these newcomers will never learn English or French.

If they never learn our language, they will never make new friends outside their ethnic community. They'll never find meaningful work. They'll never become fully Canadian.

It will take enormous effort from every Canadian — particularly our political leaders who engineered the whole situation — to ensure that the Syrian refugee story has a happy ending.

We all need to remind Justin Trudeau that his promise to these new Canadians is not delivered with hugs and selfies at Pearson Airport. It will not be delivered until the newest Syrian refugees and their children embrace their Canadian classmates on soccer fields, at school concerts and at graduation ceremonies across the country.

Engagement, pluralism and integration are the opposite of the hands-off approach of Europe's state-led multiculturalism, which has been an unmitigated failure.

After decades of ignored warnings, European multiculturalism was finally condemned by such leaders as Britain's David Cameron and Germany's Angela Merkel just as social breakdown is erupting in crisis.

Canadians must do everything in our power to not allow this catastrophe to repeat itself here. Trudeau must not be given the option of reverting back to his father's policy of official multiculturalism.

His government must be encouraged to continue the work of Stephen Harper and Jason Kenney to replace multiculturalism with pluralism.

That is why the current dynamic of refugee resettlement workers asking Trudeau for a "pause" is particularly bothersome. We should be ringing the alarm bell and demanding better of our politicians.

Little Mogadishu on the Prairies

While Canada has done much better than Europe when it comes to resettlement and integration, we do not have a perfect track record. In fact, we are repeating many of the refugee resettlement mistakes made by the previous Liberal administration under Jean Chrétien.

Much like the ongoing crisis in Syria today, starting in the late 1980s, Somalia was engaged in a deadly civil war that lasted for nearly three decades. Canada led the world's efforts with its generous pledge to resettle Somali refugees through the UNHCR.

Canada now has one of the largest Somali diasporas in the West, with approximately 150,000 residents. But it has not been a refugee success story. Since Somalis fled the civil war and found refuge in Canada, the result has at times been anything but positive. The community is marred by unemployment, crime and isolation.

A recent study found that upwards of 80 per cent of the Somali population in Canada relies on social services and social welfare due to a lack of education, skills or employment, all of which stem from a lack of language proficiency. Most Somalis in Canada do not speak French or English and therefore have not integrated or found stable work.[21]

Instead, these former refugees — who by and large were brought in by the government-assisted program, rather than through private sponsorship — remain dependent on government handouts and are relegated to isolated communities, in the suburbs of Toronto, Ottawa, Calgary and Vancouver, as well as in Fort McMurray, Alberta.

More than 50 young Somali men were murdered over the past decade in Ontario and Alberta alone. This includes the high-profile 2012 shooting at the Eaton Centre in Toronto, when Ahmed Hassan, Nixon Nirmalendran, and Christopher Husbands engaged in an open gunfight in the crowded food court on a busy Saturday afternoon.

Hassan, a Somali-born Toronto gang member, was wanted on drug-related charges in Fort McMurray. Both Hassan and Nirmalendran died in the shootout, which left several others wounded, including a 13-year-old boy who was struck by a stray bullet.

In the Vancouver suburb of Surrey, an organization that works directly with Somali refugees is focused almost entirely on preventing young Somalis from joining gangs. "It's a big problem generally in the youth," said Amos Kambere, executive director of the Umoja Operation Compassion Society of B.C. "These people are coming with issues of trauma, issues of mental health and when they come here they are overwhelmed."[22]

According to the group, there were 23 shootings in just two months during the summer of 2015. And according to the RCMP, these shootings are connected to an ongoing turf war between Somali and South Asian gangs.

Here is a community that has not integrated. It has remained segregated and isolated. The sad reality is that this is Canada's failure. We did not work hard enough or employ the right resources to ensure these refugees integrated into Canadian society.

Instead, we followed the European approach and herded Somalis into isolated silos, where they formed parallel societies.

Today most young Somali men, including those born in Canada, have difficulty finishing school. They struggle with the Canadian curriculum. They receive very little educational support at home. They often come from homes where nobody can speak, read or write in English and nobody has graduated from high school. They in turn do not have the skills to find employment. Instead, many turn to gangs and drug trafficking. This is a deadly cycle that engulfs Somalis, regardless of where in Canada they settle.

Of course, not all Somalis are criminals. Not all Somalis are stuck in the dependency trap. There are encouraging stories of Somalis who have become role models in their communities and have made tremendous contributions to Canadian society.

But even the most successful among them, Grammy award-winning singer, poet and rapper K'naan, acknowledges the severe problems facing his community in Canada. In an interview with the CBC, K'naan talked about how he copes with the violence and murder within his community. He was asked if he's lost more friends and family to violence in Toronto than he did in Somalia. "No," he responded, "but it's rivalling."

K'naan, like many other Somalis, suffers from post-traumatic stress disorder from his experiences in the Somali civil war. And while he says he appreciates his life and the opportunities he was given in Canada, he believes that Somalis don't do very well here. Studies back up this view. A 2013 report from York University found that "a lack of language proficiency and professional training" have resulted in significant poverty levels among the Somali community in Canada.[23]

Somalis suffered tremendous atrocities in a war, followed by violence and discrimination in UN refugee camps, only to face an enormous culture shock when they arrived in Canada. They were in great need of support from Canada's refugee resettlement agencies, which were not adequately prepared to help.

Some Somalis didn't just bring their trauma, mental health issues and distress over to Canada: some also brought existing feuds and gang rivalries. They were not stopped from importing their violence and are today still participating in crime in Canada just as they did in Somalia.

While some of the blame for the problems of the Somali community in Canada can and should be leveled against the Chrétien government, many of this community's struggles are internal and self-perpetuating.

It turns out that the U.S. and Europe both face disproportionate crime and terrorism from their Somali diasporas. Just look at the crime rate or poverty levels in the Minneapolis neighbourhood of Cedar Riverside, also known as Little Mogadishu, to get an idea of the problem. According to a report from the Minneapolis Star Tribune, "the number of Somali adults and children who participated in the state's family cash assistance program jumped 34 per cent from 2008 to 2013, to 5,950. At the same time, food assistance participation increased 98 per cent, to 17,300 adults and children, which does not include U.S.-born Somalis."[24]

If the poverty ensnaring refugee populations is a grave concern, radicalization and Islamist fascism is even more troubling.

It may seem counter-intuitive to hear that Minnesota is the U.S.'s largest source of foreign fighters who have gone overseas to fight with radical Islamic organizations. But knowing that Cedar Riverside hosts the largest concentration of Somalis in the U.S. helps understand the terror connection.

Likewise, a recent segment of 60 Minutes Australia captures a terrifying moment when a film crew in Sweden is attacked by masked men in a no-go zone also dubbed Little Mogadishu. This is a troubling trend when it comes to Somali diasporas, whether in Canada, the U.S. or Europe. These communities have great difficulty adapting to western liberal societies.

I am hopeful and optimistic that, over time, the vast majority of Canadians in the Somali community will adapt to life in the West, that one day, Somali-Canadians will come to champion freedom and the rule of law. But this transition will not happen automatically or overnight.

It will take a sustained effort to overcome the ingrained attitudes and behaviours these people have learned from life in Somalia and refugee camps. We hope Somalis will integrate into Canadian society. We believe that they can. But hoping and believing are not enough.

Canada was generous in admitting refugees from Somalia, but saying yes to refugees is the just the first step in a long and challenging process. We all need to work harder — both government and civil society — to help this struggling community to integrate into Canadian society.

Radicalized Migrants and the Homegrown Threat

Studies repeatedly show that how newcomers are treated when they arrive in their host country largely dictates how successful that person will be.[25]

This pivotal moment for Canada's Syrian refugees was squandered simply because Justin Trudeau agreed to bring in more refugees than our institutions had the capacity to manage.

Neglect and isolation can drive people already prone to radicalization to foster a hatred for the West. Some will be more easily recruited into radical networks.

There is a long history of disenfranchised refugees, young men and increasingly young women, picking up arms against their host country.

Al-Shabaab, a faction of al-Qaeda operating in North Africa, was formed in the UN refugee camps in Somalia. Its name, which means "The Youth," comes from these early origins, when the group was essentially a youth wing of al-Qaeda and its Islamic recruiting arm amongst those fleeing the Somali civil war.

The early leaders of the Taliban, one of the most ruthless and oppressive organizations on the planet, formed of men fleeing the Russians in Afghanistan. These refugees were educated and trained, indeed radicalized and brainwashed, while in refugee camps in Pakistan.

The Boston Marathon bombers were asylum seekers and landed refugees; the two brothers were radicalized and became fanatic Islamists as young men living in the United States. Growing up a six-minute drive from Harvard, the younger brother, Dzhokhar Tsarnaev was enrolled in marine biology at the University of Massachusetts Dartmouth. But he had failed seven courses and was deeply in debt to the university after failing to pay his tuition.[26]

Likewise, the Daesh terrorists who attacked Paris in late 2015 were all European Union nationals, who were either migrants themselves or the children of migrants. They were recruited, radicalized and trained in the E.U., under the noses of intelligence officials in Belgium and France.

In Canada, we know of several radical Islamists who were either radicalized in Canada, or came to Canada as radicalized refugees or immigrants.

Take Hiva Alizadeh, for instance, who came to Canada as a refugee from Iran in 2002. In 2010, he was arrested for a terrorist plot that would have included blowing up Parliament. He had pledged allegiance to al-Qaeda, travelled to Afghanistan to attend a terrorist training camp, built homemade bombs and IEDs and was part of the terrorist cell in Ottawa. In 2014, Alizadeh pled guilty to terrorist-related charges and is now serving his sentence in a Canadian jail.[27]

Alizadeh was part of what the Canadian Security Intelligence Service (CSIS) calls a "terror cluster" — a group of jihadists who work towards deadly attacks while recruiting new members into their fold. CSIS has warned that such terror clusters likely exist in every major Canadian city.[28]

Fortunately, Canada has been able to thwart several terrorist plots. The most memorable was the arrest in 2006 of the Toronto 18.

This homegrown terror cell consisted of 18 young Muslim immigrants, refugees and the sons of immigrants and refugees from Afghanistan, Pakistan, Jordan, Egypt, Saudi Arabia, Iraq and Somalia.

The ringleader, Zakaria Amara, is a Jordanian who had moved to Canada as a teenager and became a citizen as a young adult. By the age of 20, he was arrested and facing a laundry list of terrorism-related charges and eventual convictions.

Amara had assembled a team and begun working on a terrifying plot.

They planned to blow up the Toronto Stock Exchange, go on shooting sprees in downtown Toronto and storm the CBC headquarters on Front Street. Meanwhile, they would also lay siege to Parliament Hill in Ottawa and behead politicians and leaders of each party. For a grand finale, they wanted to force Prime Minister Stephen Harper to his knees and behead him on national television.

These men were well on their way to carrying out this unthinkable massacre: they rented a warehouse and had already received shipments of three tons of ammonium-nitrate fertilizer to be used in making powerful bombs.

The plot was intercepted thanks only to the excellent work of the RCMP's anti-terrorist squad, including a Muslim undercover agent who attended the same Mississauga mosque as Toronto 18 members. Following a sting operation, the men were arrested and charged.

Despite the fact that all 18 men were Muslim migrants — they all attended the same mosque, were radicalized by the same imam, and had all participated in paramilitary training at rural Ontario outposts — several media outlets failed to mention religion or terrorism as a motive.

The Toronto Star wrote that it was "difficult to find a common denominator" amongst the men.[29]

The New York Times described the men as coming from "broad strata of our society."[30]

What a farce. No wonder many Canadians no longer trust mainstream media outlets to deliver factual news.

The Toronto 18 were by no means the only instance of Islamist terror plots within Canada.

More recently, the RCMP and CSIS intercepted an al-Qaeda-affiliated plot to derail a train travelling from New York City to Toronto. Both of the terrorist conspirators in this incident, known as the Via Rail plot, were Muslim migrants to Canada.

Chiheb Esseghaier is a Tunisian who came to Canada on a student visa, while Palestinian Raed Jaser entered Canada illegally in 1993 using a fake passport. The Canadian government tried to deport Jaser after he was convicted of fraud and uttering threats, but was unable to do so due to his "stateless" status.[31]

While many of the terror threats facing Canada come from radicalized migrants, there is also a growing concern over homegrown terrorism.

Migration and the flow of peoples is often a two-way street. While we should worry that Canada may be importing jihadists alongside refugees from Syria, we should also be concerned about Canadians leaving to join the terrorists elsewhere — and the threat of their eventual return.

These Canadian foreign fighters, whether Canadian citizens, Muslim migrants or recent Muslim-converts, get further radicalized, desensitized and extensively trained abroad.

Take, for instance, 23-year-old Abu Turaab, formerly known as Mohammed Ali. According to a comprehensive report by the National Post's Stewart Bell, the Canadian citizen left Mississauga, Ontario to join Daesh in April 2014.[32] He became a prominent propaganda agent, using social media to recruit new fighters, praise terrorist attacks and motivate Muslims to become jihadists. His Twitter account was suspended multiple times after he threatened Canada and posted photos of Daesh fighters holding severed heads.[33]

After Daesh brutally beheaded a captured U.S. soldier, the Canadian tweeted that he wanted to play soccer with the decapitated head. He made the same joke after Daesh beheaded American journalist James Foley.[34]

Is Canada ready for the day this monster decides to return home?

Or what about John Maguire, who changed his name to Abu Anwar al-Canadi upon moving to Syria and joining Daesh. Maguire received significant news coverage when he starred in a Daesh propaganda video in late 2014. Standing in the ruins of an unidentified town in Syria or Iraq, donning a head scarf and holding an assault rifle, the convert criticizes Muslims in Canada for not joining Daesh. He threatens all Canadians, saying we have no right to live in safety.[35]

"It should not surprise you when operations by the Muslims are executed where it hurts you the most — on your very own soil," he said in the video. "Your people will be indiscriminately targeted, as you indiscriminately target our people."[36]

Maguire grew up in the small Ontario community of Kemptville and studied at the University of Ottawa, where he got involved with the Muslim students' association. In the video, he says he grew up "on the hockey rink," excelled in school and had no criminal record. He then converted to Islam and soon became the radicalized and hateful man we saw in the video.

These are just two of the many young men and women who have left Canada to join Daesh's ranks in Syria and Iraq.

When CSIS released its terrorist watch list at the start of 2016,[37] the numbers were alarming.

There were 180 Canadians known to be fighting with terrorist groups abroad, up from around 120 in 2015. The number of foreign fighters — Canadians who travelled to the Middle East and North Africa to join terrorist forces — had grown by 50 per cent. The number of those fighting for Daesh had more than tripled.

Can we take solace in assuming that these young Islamist zealots are taking their war elsewhere, and will likely be killed in the field? Or should we be worried about the day they return to Canada, educated and trained by the world's deadliest jihadists?

The same CSIS report revealed that Canadian security officials know of at least 60 foreign fighters who are now back in Canada.

How did they escape Daesh's tight grip, which forbids its fighters from leaving? Perhaps they didn't escape. Maybe they were sent back to Canada on assignment.

The phenomenon of foreign fighters is not unique to Canada. There are as many as 31,000 foreign fighters from nearly 100 countries who have gone to fight for Daesh in Iraq and Syria, including more than 10,000 from Europe.[38] Despite a sustained international effort to stem the flow of foreign fighters, the number doubled between June 2014 and December 2015.

The rise of foreign fighters shows the ubiquitous threat of Islamist radicalization brewing throughout our society. There is a pattern emerging in both Europe and North America of the radicalization of western-born Muslims. Second generation immigrants are choosing to reject western culture and values and instead embrace a radical religion that their own parents likely rejected. Radicalization is occurring online through jihadi outreach, but also through radical imams in local mosques.

In recent years, we've seen numerous accounts of young Muslims being radicalized here in Canada.

Of course, the two most notorious examples resulted in deadly terrorist attacks against members of Canada's Armed Forces just two days apart in October 2014, described in the first chapter.

First, Martin Couture-Rouleau — a radicalized Quebecer and Muslim convert — intentionally rammed his car into two officers, killing Warrant Officer Patrice Vincent before dying in a shootout with police.[39] Couture-Rouleau was being monitored by authorities after he pledged allegiance to Daesh; in July 2014 he was arrested at the airport, had his passport seized and was stopped from boarding a plane to Turkey.

And then, just two days later, the son of a Libyan radical attacked the nation's capital. Michael Zehaf-Bibeau gunned down Cpl. Nathan Cirillo before storming Centre Block, shooting a guard and ultimately being killed by the sergeant-at-arms.

Despite the media's preferred description of Zehaf-Bibeau as a "lone wolf," the man had connections to other terrorists in Canada, including one who went overseas to fight with Daesh. The RCMP were aware of his troubled past, and began investigating him when he applied for a passport. Zehaf-Bibeau wanted to join the civil in Libya.[40]

Both these terrorists wished to travel overseas to carry out their jihad. They are not alone.

In February 2015, reports surfaced of seven Quebec teens and young adults who left home and are believed to have joined Daesh.[41] Two more teens were arrested in April that same year and faced terrorism-related charges. A month later, 10 young Montrealers were intercepted at the airport and stopped from boarding a plane, allegedly on their way to joining Daesh.[42]

What is driving these youngsters to leave comfortable lives in the suburbs and join a tribal war? And how do second-generation Muslim teenagers end up embracing a violent and radical ideology their parents reject?

We know that much of Daesh's allure comes from its social media propaganda, but it's also worth examining the families and communities these radicalized youths leave behind.

In November 2014, a 20-year-old student from Alabama told her parents she was going on a school trip to Atlanta. Instead, Hoda Muthana boarded a plane to Turkey, met up with friends she'd made on social media and illegally crossed the border into Syria to join Daesh. She became a so-called "jihadi bride" — a woman who gets assigned to marry a jihadi, when he blows himself up or dies in action she gets reassigned to another man.[43]

Muthana's father is a deeply religious man who encouraged his daughter to peacefully study the Qur'an. He fled Yemen with his wife to give their children a better life, free of the violence and civil war that plagues much of the Middle East — violence and a civil war, ironically, that his daughter is now embracing.

"I want to apologize for what my daughter did," the shamed man said in an interview. The Muslim community in their hometown has also taken a direct stance. On the home page of the Birmingham Islamic Society's website, there's an open letter denouncing the Islamic State's poisonous ideology. It uses a religious argument to condemn terrorism:

"Those who commit acts of terror, murder and cruelty in the name of Islam are not only destroying innocent lives, but are also betraying the values of the faith they claim to represent."

The Muslim community in Birmingham has even taken out paid advertisements in local newspapers to share their anti-terrorism message. They want everyone — Muslims and non-Muslims alike — to know that their community condemns violence. Full stop. Now juxtapose the Birmingham Society's response with that of Montreal Imam Adil Charkaoui.

Charkaoui teaches Arabic and Qur'an studies at a community centre in East Montreal; several of the young Muslims who have joined or tried to join Daesh formerly attended his classes.[44]

Charkaoui's background raises serious questions. In 2003, He was arrested on a security certificate after the "millennium bomber" Ahmed Ressan told authorities that Charkaoui attended an al-Qaeda training camp and was a threat to Canadian national security.[45] According to a report by Martin Patriquin in Maclean's, he spent 21 months in jail and was considered an al-Qaeda "sleeper agent," who was planning a deadly attack in Canada. Charkaoui denied the allegations and was never charged. Ressan later recanted his story and the case against Charkaoui was deemed unconstitutional. Charkaoui was eventually given Canadian citizenship.

Charkaoui has denied that his teachings at the community centre are radicalizing students and has accused Quebec politicians of being "agents of radicalization" for even questioning why some of his students are becoming terrorists.

In Alabama, a grieving father who lost his daughter to a death cult shows remorse, guilt and sorrow for her decision. He isn't afraid to condemn her life choices. His community echoes this sentiment and uses every opportunity possible to show the distinction between peaceful everyday Muslims and the radical sects that disgrace their religion.

In Canada, Adil Charkaoui calls Canadian politicians "agents of radicalization" for asking questions. This is unhelpful, both to Muslims trying to separate themselves from radical Islam, and to a country trying to come to terms with the new phenomenon of homegrown terrorism.

There is no proof that Adil Charkaou is a terrorist, but it is reasonable to ask questions about what is going on in his classroom. This is not a far-reaching demand.

The Montreal example is not the only one. There are similar cases across the country and indeed around the world. Canada needs to demand answers from imams, particularly those with a history of extremism.

Look at the case of Imam Aly Hindy and his role as leader of a mosque attended by the members of the Toronto 18. The controversial Egyptian-born religious leader has been involved in all kinds of controversy, from presiding over polygamous marriage ceremonies to defending those convicted of terrorism.

Hindy is still the imam of the Salaheddin Islamic Centre in Toronto, despite his notable connections to fundamentalists or the fact that his centre has received significant donations over the years from authoritarian regimes such as Qatar and Saudi Arabia.[46]

Canada allows all of this to happen while barely raising an eyebrow. These Islamists promote and advance their illiberal ideas by exploiting Canada's freedoms.

Don't hold your breath waiting for things to improve under Justin Trudeau. Our prime minister simply isn't interested in giving serious scrutiny to these radicals.

Trudeau ignores the hateful message coming from the mosques he visits. He whitewashes the religious motivations from any discussion of terrorism and national security.

If a Christian or Conservative leader said anything close to the odious and intolerant remarks coming from these fundamentalist mosques — about gay marriage, spousal abuse or religious superiority — Trudeau would no doubt hold a dramatic press conference to denounce them.

But when it comes to Muslim communities in Canada — a key part of his voting coalition — Trudeau is willing to turn a blind eye to the brewing storm of Islamic intolerance and radicalism.

When he ignores the growing evidence of radical Islamist insurgency he puts the lives of all Canadians at risk. Including and especially the lives of Muslims who are peaceful and loyal to Canada.

Silos of Illiberalism

Isolated cultural and linguistic neighbourhoods can become breeding grounds for resentment and radicalism. The potent mix of populations prone to a radical religious ideology, and the failed integration policies of western Liberals has allowed their creation

The long-term challenges that come along with the changing makeup of our population include a formidable security threat. The immediate risk of an impending terrorist attack is pressing and disconcerting, and yet, the long-term risks to our society, even our civilization, is perhaps a greater worry.

The Trudeau government is not doing enough to ensure we do not fall victim to the same mistakes as Europe. We must not import Europe's formula — and its deadly consequences — to Canada.

The most severe consequence of Trudeau's open-door-to-Syrians policy may well be the formation of Daesh and al-Qaeda cells throughout North America. It's already happened in Europe, thanks to decades of wrong-headed policies.

The no-go zones in and around Paris have become notorious for their anti-Semitism and violence, and, increasingly, as the base for radical Islamists and the launching place for their attacks. These neighbourhoods are isolated, intolerant to outsiders, governed by strict Sharia and bankrolled by Wahhabis in Saudi Arabia.

French civil society is defined by its secular liberalism and a fierce commitment to the legal equality of men and women. But migrants whose own views are the antithesis of progressive French society were left isolated and unchallenged. This comes from decades of a vivre et laisser vivre — live and let live — policy when it came to newcomers.

France is certainly not alone. Germany has spent the past half-century apologizing for its crimes during the Second World War and has had great trouble assuming any kind of national identity since. Germans, therefore, tiptoe around any newcomer's intolerance and try their best to be accommodating. Thanks to its own illiberal history, it is difficult for Germans to be critical of the illiberal traditions of many Muslim cultures.

Instead, when newcomers arrive, they are not asked to change a thing about themselves. They are not asked to learn the language, adapt to German culture or codes of conduct, or be patriotic to national institutions. Even the German flag, a nondescript tricolor of red, black and gold that was introduced in 1949 after the war, has become a sign of supposed neo-nationalism. Some German politicians refuse to wave German flags at rallies.

Patriotism, a love for one's country, has become a faux pas in the dystopia of modern Europe. Instead, the fantasy of multiculturalism, that all cultures are inherently praiseworthy and deserving of equal standing, still lives on.

And consequently, there is now a third generation of Turkish descent living in Germany. They are not citizens. They do not speak German.

Steps are being taken to award citizenship to the German-born Turks, but the government still makes no attempt to encourage them to learn German or integrate into society.

According to news reports, the government's plan to engage these young German-born Turks … is to encourage more Germans to speak Turkish.

After failing for half a century to integrate Turks, Germans are now simply giving in and learning Turkish instead.[47]

So the mass sexual assaults that occurred in Cologne and many other cities across Europe on New Year's Eve 2015 are a shocking development, but a not surprising one.

In the final hours of 2015, and the first few of 2016, there were more than 500 reported sexual assaults in Cologne — a city smaller than Calgary.

Police reports described a chaotic and frightening scene. Officers were vastly outnumbered by the aggressive young men who gathered in Cathedral Square and an adjacent train station. Police felt helpless as "distraught, crying, frightened" women were forced to run a gauntlet of aggressive and violent young men described as "North African and Arab."

The reports describe how "security forces were unable to get all the incidents, assaults, crimes, etc. under control. There were just too many happening at the same time."

The leaked police report went on to confirm the involvement of many of the same migrants that German Chancellor Angela Merkel had welcomed in the previous weeks and months. Despite many officials claiming that no refugees were involved, first-hand accounts paint a different picture.

Some of the attackers were directly provoking police officers on the scene. "I'm Syrian, you must treat me kindly," one man said to police. "Ms. Merkel invited me here." Another tore up his German residency papers, and grinned at police, saying they could no longer arrest him. "I'll just go back and get a new one," he smugly told them.

Despite the mass chaos and an apparent breakdown of law and order, the official government report was glowing.

The Cologne police department issued a news release the following day calling the New Year's Eve festivities "relaxed" and "peaceful."

German officials were walking on eggshells, trying to avoid fueling anti-refugee sentiment. So they at first suppressed reports of the mass refugee-on-German sexual assaults that took place.

Even as reports began surfacing — leaked police reports, cell phone videos and first-hand accounts — many German officials continued to deny the accusations that refugees had carried out these crimes against German girls and women.

The mayor of Cologne, Henriette Reker, in an ugly act of victim-blaming, told German girls to follow a "code of conduct" in public and to "stay at arm's length" from strange men.[48]

This would be laughable, if it weren't so reflective of the times. Of course, when an angry mob of sexually repressed and drunk young men surround you in a public square, then tear at your clothes and violently molest you, rob you, and, if they can, rape you, it's difficult to adhere to such a "code of conduct."

But this is just the latest example of a barbaric cultural practice that has been imported from the Middle East alongside migrants.

There is even an Arabic name for this phenomenon; one that reveals that violent attackers consider it a game. It's known as *taharrush gamea,* or collective sex, and it was on full display to the West during the Tahir square mob protests in Cairo during the Arab Spring.

The most prominent victim was NBC reporter Lara Logan. In the midst of the chaos and crowds at large public gatherings, young men encircle an unsuspecting woman, while an outer circle of men stops any rescuers. They tear the woman away from her husband, boyfriend, friends, brother or father, then hold her down, tear off her clothes, and take turns raping her. In Egypt, this is commonplace and is even used by security forces as a tactic against female protesters. That's what women get for leaving the house in an Arab country.

In liberal democratic Germany, however, women and men are supposed to enjoy equal rights. But some misogynistic newcomers just can't help themselves. They were raised to believe that women were property.

They saw how German civil society was bending over backwards to accommodate them. They were never told to become German or even be respectful of German traditions. And after they committed these sexual crimes in Cologne and elsewhere, German officials went out of their way to deny the crimes and cover up for the migrant. So why would these young men change their ways?

Officials first covered up the facts, then they tried to deny that refugees were involved, then they made excuses for the perpetrators by saying it wasn't their fault; they just didn't know it was wrong to assault women. Why would they? No one ever told them that things were different in Europe. They were never told to adopt western liberal standards of liberty and equality.

German Chancellor Angela Merkel and other European leaders have lost control of their refugee crisis. The tide of public opinion has shifted, as we can see with the rise of anti-immigration sentiment on both the political left and the right.

The reality is that large numbers of the refugees streaming into Europe — which heavily skew male; upwards of 65 per cent registered in Greece and Italy were men[49] — were raised in misogynistic madrassas and hold values that are simply incompatible with liberal democracies. Those who reject our western laws and values, those who see women as inferior sex objects, should not be welcomed in the first place.

This is why both Merkel and British Prime Minister David Cameron declared back in 2011 that multiculturalism has been a failed experiment. But sadly, despite this revelation, little has changed. Europe still asks nothing of newcomers, it tiptoes around the awkward subject of the barbaric cultural practices of some newcomers and it treats all Muslim migrants as victims of European social and economic oppression. Even the ones who just arrived.

This approach has brought Europe to the brink of an imported civil war. Europe has decayed into a fractured and broken society. The backlash against European leaders and open-border migration has been staunch and widespread — across the political spectrum. While the loudest concerns come from those on the right, there is an equally fervent movement from the political left over concerns of an overburdened welfare state and a worry over the collapse of western liberal progress.[50] In Europe, the refugee debate transcends traditional left-right politics.[51]

Europe is dealing with a new and volatile political climate. The continent is in paralysis; enacting contradictory policies intended to both keep migrants out, as well as welcome them with no strings attached.

Meanwhile, Europe's opposing bureaucracies and labour laws mean that many newcomers and migrants are forced to live on welfare because their asylum visas require them to wait, sometimes for years, before getting work permits.[52]

Many are given application dates to apply for work permits, but must wait several years for an appointment. Navigating this Kafkaesque and ever-changing bureaucracy is a daunting task.

Europe's security and intelligence forces, the ones in charge of stopping terrorist attacks, are famously incompetent. These organizations clash and often compete with one another rather than working together.

Europe's own incompetence and competing interests are driving it towards extinction. If it cannot stop this cycle, the EU may well be the world's next failed state.

This should be a lesson for North America.

Thankfully, Canada differs from Europe in many regards. Unlike our European counterparts, Canada has not been ashamed of our history or afraid to demand that newcomers learn our language and accept our values and principles. As Europe's guilt-ridden leaders tried to distance themselves from their colonial past, and wouldn't dare ask newcomers to learn or respect their foundational traditions, Canada was taking a different approach; that of pluralism.

Newcomers to Canada are asked to become Canadian.

They enjoy freedom of religion, of conscience, of assembly and so on, but they are also asked to join our democracy, follow our rule of law and respect our rights and freedoms. No one in Canada is afraid to wave our flag or express love for our country. Canada has yet to make patriotism taboo as it is in Europe.

The Harper government specifically called out barbaric traditions and condemned illiberal practices such as female abuse, so-called honour killings, female genital mutilation, forced marriages, and domestic violence. The Conservative government explicitly told newcomers that these practices have no place in Canada.

In turn, Harper received significant blowback and ho-humming from the chattering classes, including Justin Trudeau, who thought telling some immigrants that "barbaric cultural practices" were not welcome in Canada was "too harsh."[53] It wasn't. Rather than being timid and fearful not to offend our new compatriots, the Conservatives said flat out that certain values and practices are not welcome here.

Canada's integration policy was one of the major distinctions that set us apart from other western nations. We take integration seriously and work hard to avoid the European phenomenon of migrants forming isolated cultural silos and not mixing in with the rest of society.

Simply wanting to avoid ethnic silos does not mean that we are immune to the threats of radicalization and homegrown terrorism. All of us — civil society, law enforcement, educators and the political class — must all be awake to the looming threats posed by mass migration policies.

I wrote this open letter to Syrian refugees arriving in Canada for the Toronto Sun.

While we may disagree with the reckless rush to bring 50,000 Syrian refugees here, the worst thing we can do is copy Europe in ostracizing our Muslim migrant communities. It is now the job of each individual Canadian to ensure that Muslim migrants are welcomed, engaged, integrated and accepted into mainstream civil society.

Welcome to Canada
December 9, 2015

The first wave of refugees from Syria is due to arrive in Toronto today. This is my open letter to all Syrian refugees.

Dear newcomers,

Welcome to Canada! Welcome to the greatest country in the world.

This is your home and your country now. It belongs to you just as much as it belongs to any other Canadian.

Over the days to come, you may read about the debate and disagreement regarding Canada's refugee resettlement policies, but that doesn't mean that you are not welcome here. Don't confuse the opposition to a government policy with a sentiment of being anti-refugee.

Canadians are generous and welcoming people. We open our arms to those who wish to contribute to Canadian society; those who respect and honour our traditions and help maintain our strong commitment to freedom, equality, democracy, the rule of law, peace and justice.

If you respect these values, you will do just fine here.

There is a long history of refugees playing an important role in Canadian society. As a refugee, you are not an outsider. Alongside the rights and responsibilities that come with being a Canadian, you are also encouraged to get involved in your community, meet people from other backgrounds and religions, and jump right in to Canadian life.

You can follow in the footsteps of great Canadians who started out as refugees, and rose to significant prominence in Canadian public life.

Take Rahim Jaffer, for instance. At age 25, he became the first Muslim elected to the Canadian Parliament. Jaffer was re-elected three times and in 2006 was named chair of the government caucus by former Prime Minister Stephen Harper.

Rahim Jaffer too came to Canada as a refugee. He was born in Uganda to an Ismaili Muslim family. When the ruthless dictator Idi Amin confiscated their home and their business, the Jaffer family fled from further persecution and resettled in Edmonton, Alberta.

Or look at Canada's current Minister of Democratic Institutions, Maryam Monsef, who was born in Afghanistan. When the Soviets invaded and her father was killed, her mother moved the family to Canada and they resettled in the small community of Peterborough, Ontario.

Monsef admits it was difficult at first to adapt to a new country, but once she began to learn English and get involved in the community, things got a lot better. Earlier this year, Monsef successfully ran for public office and, at age 30, she become one of the youngest cabinet ministers in Canadian history.

There is no glass ceiling for refugees in Canada.

In fact, our two most recent governors general — the representative of the Queen in Canada — Adrienne Clarkson and Michaëlle Jean were both refugees to Canada.

Refugee success stories are not limited to the political sphere. Some of Canada's most successful entrepreneurs, business leaders, and philanthropists started their Canadian journey as refugees.

Peter Munk, a well-respected Toronto businessman and generous philanthropist, fled the Nazis in Hungary as a child and resettled in Canada. Robert Herjavec, famous for his role as an investor in the TV shows Dragon's Den and Shark Tank, arrived in Canada at the age of eight after his family fled the former Yugoslavia to escape Josep Tito's communist regime.

Regardless of whether they were fleeing fascism, communism or religious persecution; whether they are Muslim, Jewish or Falun Gong;

and whether they resettle in downtown Toronto, suburban Winnipeg, or rural Alberta, refugees are an incredibly important asset to the Canadian family.

So to all the Syrian refugees arriving in Canada today, and to those who continue to arrive over the next few months, we wish you well on your journey to becoming a new Canadian.

This country has very high hopes for you.

---

[1] "Refugee crisis, drowned Syrian boy shift focus on election campaign," CBC News. Sept. 3, 2015. http://www.cbc.ca/news/politics/syria-migrants-canada-drowned-migrants-leaders-respond-1.3213878

[2] "Rick Hillier wants Canada to accept 50,000 refugees by end of year," Lee Berthiaume, Ottawa Citizen. Sept. 8, 2015. http://ottawacitizen.com/news/politics/the-gargoyle-hillier-wants-canada-to-accept-50000-refugees-by-end-of-year

[3] While France did not invoke Article Five in this instance, it could have and may do so in future.

[4] "Paris attacks: who were the attackers?" BBC News, March 18, 2016. http://www.bbc.com/news/world-europe-34832512

[5] "EU migrant proposal aim to overhaul asylum rules," New York Times. April 6, 2016. http://www.nytimes.com/2016/04/07/world/europe/eu-migrants-asylum.html?_r=0

[6] "Canada's Syria refugee plan raises concerns of 'shortcuts,' homeland security committee hears," CBC News. Feb. 3, 2016. http://www.cbc.ca/news/politics/canada-syrian-refugee-plan-us-senate-committee-shortcuts-1.3431698

[7] "ISIS Operative: This is how we send Jihadis to Europe," BuzzFeed News. Jan. 29, 2015. http://www.buzzfeed.com/mikegiglio/isis-operative-this-is-how-we-send-jihadis-to-europe#.wx2n6K5Ed

---

[8] Readers should know, I used to work for Jason Kenney during his time as Minister of Citizenship, Immigration and Multiculturalism. I was his press secretary from 2011 to 2012, and we remain friends.

[9] "Refugee crisis: Lebanese minister warns of ISIS jihadis infiltrating Europe as migrants," International Business Times. Sept. 15, 2015. http://www.ibtimes.co.uk/refugee-crisis-lebanese-minister-warns-isis-jihadis-infiltrating-europe-migrants-1519768

[10] "One in five Syrians say Islamic State is a good thing, poll says," Washington Post. Sept. 15, 2015. https://www.washingtonpost.com/news/worldviews/wp/2015/09/15/one-in-five-syrians-say-islamic-state-is-a-good-thing-poll-says/

[11] "13 Percent of Syrian Refugees Support ISIS: Poll," clarionproject.org, http://www.clarionproject.org/analysis/13-percent-syrian-refugees-support-isispoll?utm_source=dlvr.it&utm_medium=twitter

[12] "Syrian Christian refugees persecuted," Kingston Whig Standard. Geoffrey Johnston, April 3, 2016. http://www.thewhig.com/2016/04/03/syrian-christian-refugees-persecuted

[13] "Justin Trudeau says PMO role in refugee resettlement 'disgusting'" CBC News. Oct. 9, 2016 http://www.cbc.ca/news/politics/trudeau-middle-class-tax-cut-refugees-1.3264339

[14] "A 21st Century Refugee Crisis: What are the stakes of resettlement?" Center for a Secure Free Society policy roundtable with Amb. Alberto Fernandez, retired U.S. Foreign Service; Rep. Peter Hoekstra, former Congressmen, Chariman, House Intelligence Committee (2004-2011); and Ms. Candice Malcolm, SFS international fellow and syndicated columnist. Feb. 29, 2016. http://www.securefreesociety.org/events/

[15] "ISIS stole some shiny new weapons from the Iraqi army," Memlik Pasha, Vice. July 11, 2014. http://www.vice.com/en_ca/read/isis-stole-some-shiny-new-weapons-from-the-iraqi-army-989

[16] "Syrian Refugees lukewarm on coming to Canada by December 31, official say," National Post. Dec. 3, 2015 http://news.nationalpost.com/news/world/syrian-refugees-lukewarm-on-coming-to-canada-by-december-31-officials-say

[17] "Canada's Syrian refugee plan limited to women, children and families: Unaccompanied men not included because of ongoing security concerns," CBC News. Nov. 22, 2015. http://www.cbc.ca/news/politics/canada-refugee-plan-women-children-families-1.3330185

[18] "Testimony by Laura Dawson, PhD Director of the Canadian Institute." United States Senate Committee on Homeland Security and Governmental Affairs. http://www.hsgac.senate.gov/download/testimony-dawson-2016-02-03-20k

[19] "Christian, gay, family ties to Hamas: I'll be killed if I'm deported," Laurie Segal, CNN. June 22, 2015. http://money.cnn.com/2015/06/22/news/economy/john-calvin-hamas-deported/

[20] "Syrian refugee flow to Vancouver and Ottawa temporarily halted over housing shortages," CBC News. Jan. 18, 2016. http://www.cbc.ca/news/politics/refugees-ottawa-vancouver-housing-shortage-1.3409441

[21] "Refugee Research Synthesis 2009 – 2013," Jennifer Hyndman, PhD, et al. York University, prepared for the Government of Canada Department of Citizenship and Immigration Canada. May 2014.

[22] "Surrey gang shooting show Somali youth need better support, says outreach worker," CBC News. April 30, 2015. http://www.cbc.ca/news/canada/british-columbia/surrey-gang-shootings-show-somali-youth-need-better-support-says-outreach-worker-1.3055917

[23] "Refugee Research Synthesis 2009 – 2013," Jennifer Hyndman, PhD, et al. York University prepared for the Government of Canada Department of Citizenship and Immigration Canada. May 2014.

[24] "Before Welcoming Thousands of Syrian Refugees, We Should Consider What Somali Immigrants Have Brought the U.S," National Review. Sept. 11, 2015. http://www.nationalreview.com/article/423902/welcoming-thousands-syrian-refugees-we-should-consider-what-somali-immigrants-have

[25] "Refugee Research Synthesis 2009 – 2013," Jennifer Hyndman, PhD, et al. York University prepared for the Government of Canada Department of Citizenship and Immigration Canada. May 2014.

[26] "UMass Dartmouth seeks an exception to release Tsarnaev's records," Boston Globe. May 4, 2013. http://www.bostonglobe.com/metro/2013/05/03/umass-dartmouth-establish-independent-task-force-review-policies/53DDPTDDm068LXgNLyVBKL/story.html

[27] "Parliament was the terror target: expert," Ottawa Citizen. Aug. 26, 2016. http://www.ottawacitizen.com/news/Parliament+terror+target+expert/3451550/story.html

[28] "Terror cells suspected in Canada," Toronto Sun. Jan 21, 2011. http://www.torontosun.com/news/canada/2011/01/22/16990841.html

[29] "The ties that bind 17 suspects?" Toronto Star, Surya Bhattacharya, et al. June 4, 2006.

[30] "The Elephant in the Room: The mainstream media continue to suppress the "Islam" in Islamic terrorism," Andrew C. McCarthy, National Review Online Archive. June 5, 2006. https://web.archive.org/web/20060616004246/http://article.nationalreview.com/?q=MmRjMThlNDA0YmNmZWU1NzM4MGQ0NmVkOTUwMzExZTA=

[31] "Canada tried, failed to deport VIA Rail terror suspect nine years ago," Stewart Bell, National Post. April 25, 2013. http://news.nationalpost.com/news/canada/exclusive-canada-tried-failed-to-deport-via-rail-terror-suspect-nine-years-ago

[32] "Canadian Jihadist Unmasked," Stewart Bell, National Post. http://news.nationalpost.com/features/canadian-isis-fighter-abu-turaab-identified-as-mohammed-ali

[33] *Ibid*

[34] "Canadian IS Jihadist wants to 'play soccer' with heads of US decapitated soldiers," International Business Times. Sept. 17, 2014. http://www.ibtimes.com.au/canadian-jihadist-wants-play-soccer-heads-us-decapitated-soldiers-1370432

[35] "Ottawa man urges attacks on Canadians in purported ISIS video," CTV News. Dec. 7, 2014. http://www.ctvnews.ca/world/ottawa-man-urges-attacks-on-canadians-in-purported-isis-video-1.2136780

[36] *Ibid*

[37] "The Foreign Fighters Phenomenon and Related Security Trends in the Middle East," Canadian Security Intelligence Service. Jan. 1, 2016. https://www.csis-scrs.gc.ca/pblctns/wrldwtch/2016/20160129-en.php

[38] "Foreign Fighters: An Updated Assessment on the Flow of Foreign Fighters into Syria and Iraq," The Soufan Group. Dec. 2015. http://soufangroup.com/wp-content/uploads/2015/12/TSG_ForeignFightersUpdate3.pdf

[39] "Michael Zehaf-Bibeau and Martin Couture-Rouleau: their shared traits," CBC News. Oct. 27, 2014. http://www.cbc.ca/news/canada/michael-zehaf-bibeau-and-martin-couture-rouleau-their-shared-traits-1.2812241

[40] "Who is Michael Zehaf-Bibeau, the man behind the deadly Ottawa attack?" CNN. October 22, 2014. http://www.cnn.com/2014/10/22/world/canada-shooter/

[41] "Syrian jihadists believed to have recruited 6 young Quebecers," CBC. Feb. 26, 2015. http://www.cbc.ca/news/canada/montreal/syrian-jihadists-updates-from-syria-1.3406716

[42] "10 Montreal young people arrested on suspicion of wanting to join jihad," CBC News. May 19, 2015. http://www.cbc.ca/news/canada/montreal/10-montreal-young-people-arrested-on-suspicion-of-wanting-to-join-jihad-1.3079873

[43] "Girl Gone: an interview with an American in ISIS," Ellie Hall, Buzzfeed News. April 17, 2015. http://www.buzzfeed.com/ellievhall/gone-girl-an-interview-with-an-american-in-isis#.iiGzEO5YG

[44] "Adil Charkaoui: the angriest man in Montreal," Martin Patriquin, Maclean's. May 27, 2015. http://www.macleans.ca/news/canada/adil-charkaoui-the-angriest-man-in-montreal/

[45] "Man freed in 2009 was sleeper agent and terror threat, feds allege," Martin Patriquin, Maclean's. May 9, 2013. http://www.macleans.ca/news/canada/man-freed-in-2009-was-sleeper-agent-and-terror-threat-feds-allege/

[46] "Toronto's million dollar 'radical mosque,'" Stewart Bell, National Post. Feb. 16, 2012. http://news.nationalpost.com/news/canada/aly-hindy-salaheddin-islamic-centre

[47] "Reverse Integration: Germans learn Turkish to promote understanding," De Spiegel International. May 31, 2012. http://www.spiegel.de/international/germans-try-integrating-with-turkish-migrant-population-a-835653.html

[48] "Cologne Mayor's 'arm's length' advice on sexual attacks stirs outcry," Melissa Eddy, New York Times. Jan. 6, 2016. http://www.nytimes.com/2016/01/07/world/europe/cologne-mayor-henriette-reker-germany-sexual-assaults.html?_r=0

[49] "Europe's Man Problem," Valerie Hudson, Politico. Jan. 5, 2016. http://www.politico.com/magazine/story/2016/01/europe-refugees-migrant-crisis-men-213500

[50] "Dutch advance socialist case against immigration," Neil Clark, The Week. Nov. 24, 2008. http://www.theweek.co.uk/25095/dutch-advance-socialist-case-against-immigration

[51] "The march of Europe's little Trumps," The Economist. Dec. 12, 2015. http://www.economist.com/news/europe/21679855-xenophobic-parties-have-long-been-ostracised-mainstream-politicians-may-no-longer-be

[52] "Asylum seekers and the right to work in the European Economic Area," Migration Watch UK Briefing Paper. http://www.migrationwatchuk.org/briefing-paper/316

[53] "Trudeau retracts 'barbaric' remarks," CBC News. March 15, 2011. http://www.cbc.ca/news/politics/trudeau-retracts-barbaric-remarks-1.985386

PART 2: TRUDEAU'S CANADA, A CAUTIONARY TALE

CHAPTER 3: REDEFINING CANADA

What Does it Mean to be Canadian?

Following his autumn 2015 election victory, while basking in his newfound international celebrity, Canada's 23rd Prime Minister Justin Trudeau did a victory lap around the world.

Much like the love-struck Canadian media, journalists worldwide, from Turkey to the Philippines, were smitten by Canada's hip and progressive new prime minister. His illustrious pedigree and great hair certainly helped sell papers and summon page clicks.

It's always a bit surprising when Canadian politics gets international news coverage, but Trudeau has a knack for making headlines. From an obscure story about his family on the front page of a newspaper in Israel, to a red-carpet reception in Washington, D.C., Trudeau enjoys a staggering international name recognition — and a very favourable public perception — after just a few months in office.

In Canada, many of us know our prime minister a little better. Much of that shine has steadily worn away. Back home, Trudeau is known to go off script and occasionally say something so contentious, so stupid, so offside with the Canadian public that we sit dumbfounded as he walks back and offers a mea culpa.

Canadians accepted his apologies, for instance, after Trudeau said that Quebecers were "better than the rest of Canada" and that the country suffers when people from Alberta are in charge.[1]

When asked if Canada was better served when more people from Quebec than Alberta are in charge, Trudeau replied, "I'm a Liberal, so of course I think so, yes."

This is also the guy who said he admires China because its "basic dictatorship" allows the government to control the economy. What can I say; Canadians are kind and forgiving people.

During his first international media soiree, Trudeau continued to get away with this sort of babble gaff, with little scrutiny.

Trudeau did an interview with the New York Times for a piece that would be called "Trudeau's Canada, Again," with the subheading, "With support from President Obama and the legacy of his father on his side, Justin Trudeau sets out to redefine what it means to be Canadian."[2]

Read that again, and let the words soak in. With support from President Obama, Trudeau sets out to redefine what it means to be Canadian. There is so much wrong with this tactless statement, even for Liberals like Trudeau.

One might wonder, for instance, what the heck does Barack Obama have to do with Canadian identity? Why would a prime minister need the support of the American president to do anything domestically?

Worst of all, does Trudeau really think he can redefine Canada's national identity? Since when does our Canadian identity have anything to do with a politician in Ottawa? Liberals wish they had this kind of control over our country. Luckily, it's just a superficial fantasy of the political left: that society can be planned and designed by elites.

This sort of arrogance, unfortunately, has become commonplace and acceptable amongst political and media elites in Canada. It merely echoes the mantra repeated ad nauseam by the Trudeau government when they say that "Canada is back."

As if Canada ever went away.

Smugness aside, it is icky, it is fundamentally incorrect, and it's plain un-Canadian to suggest that politicians in Ottawa and Washington have a hand in defining or redefining what it means to be Canadian.

Despite what self-important politicians and adoring journalists may believe, Canadian identity is far removed from the halls of government.

The character of our nation is distinct. It is often at odds with its political class.

I believe we can more readily define this great country by the kids playing hockey on a frozen pond in Timmins, Ontario, the curious and free-loving 20-somethings backpacking across Southeast Asia or volunteering in Africa, or family barbecues on the beach in Campbell River, B.C., than by examining the privileged upbringing of our prime minister.

Trudeau's very willingness to embrace the spotlight and exaggerate the celebrity of his role goes against the modest and prudent values held by most Canadians.

Even more so, Canada does not accept or need the support of the American president in defining our national culture or identity. It is an astonishing statement. It feels wrong on the surface to most Canadians. Indeed, the exact opposite is true. Canadians have a strong and sometimes irrational need to separate and differentiate ourselves from our American neighbours.

We do not take Canada's sovereignty lightly. The mere suggestion that we need help from the Americans — the president no less — is insulting to Canadian sensibilities.

Try the thought experiment, if you will, of how Canadians would react if you took that flippant comment from a journalist and turned it on its head.

Imagine that back in 2006, the Paper of Record wrote that new Conservative prime minister Stephen Harper and lame-duck president George W. Bush, were teaming up to change what it means to be Canadian.

Canadians would howl at the suggestion and rightly so. Every pundit and columnist would chime in to refute the idea that Canadian culture can be redefined, let alone by a couple of know-nothings like Bush and Harper.

This cool New York Times feature, of course, flew under the radar of critique as Canada's chattering classes eagerly consumed the narrative that Trudeau had ascended to restore Canada.

The handwringing over the damage done to our international reputation from nine years of Conservative rule was finally over: Canada's elites were rejoicing in the taking back of their country. Obama, after all, is cool and hip and progressive, so of course he can help Canadians to redefine our national identity.

Naturally, the silent majority of right-thinking Canadians reject the notion that Trudeau, or any politician or elected official, has *that* much power.

Our identity, much like our values and our culture, is deeply entrenched in Canada's customs and institutions. It is up to Canadians, and not the federal government, to define our Canadian identity.

According to the Time's paraphrasing of Trudeau the Younger's vision, "Canada is becoming a new kind of state, not defined by its European history but by the multiplicity of its identities from all over the world. His embrace of pan-cultural heritage makes him an avatar of his father's vision." Trudeau's plan couldn't be more clear: he rejects western values and Canadian pluralism.

Instead, he wants to bring official multiculturalism back in Canada. He sees nothing special or remarkable about Canada or its western history, and prefers to think of Canada as a hodge-podge of many cultures that are all equal.

Trudeau's most offensive remark came near the end of this piece, when he told the Times, "there is no core identity, no mainstream in Canada."

That is a stunningly naive comment. Justin Trudeau is wrong. There is a core Canadian identity.

There are mainstream Canadians values. That Trudeau cannot see this self-evident reality — after travelling the country as the son of a prime minister and then again while campaigning non-stop over five years, no less — is troubling.

Canada's culture and its values are deeply rooted in our western heritage and traditions. We are part of the legacy of the greatest civilization in human history. And while you certainly do not need to be of European ancestry to be a Canadian, you cannot deny that our free, peaceful, law-abiding and prosperous society is built upon the ideals and traditions of our British and French forefathers.

Canada didn't just happen.

We didn't get to where we are today by holding unfamiliar and illiberal traditions above our own. We are the beneficiaries of an incredibly important legacy. We can not and should not simply erase the western influence over our past. Nor can we dismissively ignore how our free society was built. It is wrong to separate our western culture and values from our history, as Trudeau seems keen to do.

Trudeau's statement is insulting to Canadian sensibilities, a sign of the low regard he has for our identity.

Trudeau, like the failed leaders of Europe, seems to believe there is nothing special about western values. And since there is nothing special about our culture, there is no point in asking newcomers to accept these values or integrate into our society. Instead, anyone can come to Canada, so goes the thinking of official multiculturalism, without changing anything about themselves. They don't need to learn our language, abide by our norms and values, or even necessarily follow our laws.

In Trudeau's diminished and misguided worldview, every culture is equal and being Canadian means nothing at all.

Just as Europe's leaders have been too embarrassed to celebrate their traditions or demand that newcomers accept their foundational principles of rights and freedoms, Trudeau, too, is trying to distance himself from Canada's past.

He'd rather call us a "pan-cultural" society than admit that Canada is an important, highly successful product of western civilization, worthy of being celebrated and honoured. This is worse than moral relativism because it deliberately condemns the West, while suggesting that foreign cultures — even those which are objectively illiberal — are equally worthy of praise. This is textbook multiculturalism. And it's exactly the kind of thinking that has devastated Europe and brought war to its doorstep.

Illiberal Liberals and Canadian Rights and Responsibilities

Let's examine Trudeau's revisionist claim that Canada is not defined by its western history.

Our system of government — a constitutional monarchy and parliamentary democracy — is closely modelled after that of our British political ancestors.

Our regard for individual liberty, equality before the law, democracy and the rule of law is a direct result of the Enlightenment era and French and British philosophy.

Our modern society embodies the principles of liberal Enlightenment thinkers such as John Locke, J.S. Mill, Adam Smith, Alexis de Tocqueville, Frederic Bastiat and David Hume, to name a few. Our tradition of liberty realizes the vision of these thinkers perhaps more than any other place on the planet.

While our American neighbours tend to make a lot more noise about their dedication to freedom, Canadians have long taken this task seriously. We have worked to enshrine our ancient liberties in the laws and institutions of our society.

For hundreds of years, settlers and immigrants have made the journey to Canada and contributed to the development of our country and the rich diversity of our society.

Regardless of where they came from, newcomers arriving in Canada faced unimaginable difficulties. They were forced to adjust to a new land and a hostile climate. Canadians have embraced this struggle because they believe in the Canadian dream and way of life.

Canadians take great pride in our national identity — which is distinct, in our eyes, from our American neighbours and European forefathers. We honour those who made tremendous sacrifices to build this great nation.

An important note here, by way of explanation: when I discuss western liberal democracy, and the liberals who imagined our free society before it came to fruition, this type of liberalism is distinct and staggeringly different from the "liberalism" practiced by Ontario and federal political Liberals in Canada.

A small-l liberal is a person who stands for individual liberty; a person who seeks to protect individuals from the tyranny and arbitrary rule of a powerful government.

Sadly, in Canada the time-honoured liberal philosophy has been co-opted by the Liberal Party of Canada, which long ago abandoned its commitment to classical liberalism in pursuit of power through an overarching and intrusive central government. [3]

Far from championing individual freedom from government, Ontario and federal Canadian Liberals want to use government power to impose so-called social justice and progressive values upon the rest of us. To quote Edmund Burke, "their liberty is not liberal."

So when I refer to classical liberalism or our western liberal democracy, I'm talking about our broad moral commitment to the principles of liberty and a free society — certainly not the Liberal Party of Canada.

Western liberal democracies are nations committed to foundational beliefs such as (but not limited to): the obligation to respect the rights and freedom of individuals; the idea that all human beings are of equal moral worth; that all citizens are equal before the law; that all citizens have the right to a fair trial with the presumption of innocence; that coercion must only be used by the state, in accordance with the rule of law; that policies are designed based on principles of fairness and reciprocity; that people should not be legally discriminated against on the basis of gender, race, religion or orientation; that legitimate government depends on the consent of the governed, where each person in society is entitled to one vote and where a government is selected through the principle of majority rules; and so on.

This bundle of valuable principles did not manifest itself in other cultures or other parts of the world. Indeed, most of the world still does not operate under the norms that we in the West have long enjoyed.

We should not be afraid to say that our traditions are the gold standard.

Everyone who does not enjoy these expansive freedoms and liberties should aspire to achieve them, and everyone who has them to fight to uphold them. Western liberal democracies are objectively better places to live. A casual look at global migration confirms this. People leave unfree countries to live in free countries. Most people, if given a chance, would rather live under Canadian laws and institutions, even considering the incredible challenges that come with migration.

Canada today stands on the shoulders of some of the world's earliest human rights defenders. They created one of the freest, fairest and most harmonious societies in human history.

Why should we, then, start importing other less-liberal values and principles to replace our own? In short, we should not.

Instead, we must resist when politicians like Justin Trudeau opine that it's desirable or even obligatory to replace our birthright with something foreign and inferior.

Contrary to Trudeau's comment to the New York Times, Canada is not simply a hodge-podge assortment of various people from various places who hold various values, some of which happen to overlap.

Canada is an incredibly proud nation — with plenty to be proud of — and holds a deeply ingrained set of shared values and commitments. From these values, Canadians derive a distinct identity, defined not by how we look, but by how we live. Our core identity is defined by the rights and responsibilities of Canadian citizenship.

All Canadians should hold dearly our rights and responsibilities, which come from our history, are secured by Canadian law, and reflect our shared traditions, identity and values.[4]

According to Discover Canada[5] — the citizenship study guide given to all aspiring new Canadians — Canadian law has several sources aside from the laws passed by Parliament, the Constitution Act, 1867, and the 1982 Charter of Rights and Freedoms. Our laws are also derived from English common law, the civil code of France and the unwritten constitution that we inherited from Great Britain. Accordingly, Canada has an 800-year-old tradition of ordered liberty, dating back to the signing of Magna Carta, the Great Charter of Freedoms, in 1215 in England.

Habeas corpus, the right to challenge unlawful detention by the state, comes from English common law. So too do these inalienable rights:

- Freedom of conscience and religion;
- Freedom of thought, belief, opinion and expression, including freedom of speech and of the press;
- Freedom of peaceful assembly; and
- Freedom of association.

You cannot have rights without corresponding responsibilities. So, when a person is about to become Canadian, we require them to read Discover Canada, which says our responsibilities include:

- Obeying the law — One of Canada's founding principles is the rule of law. Individuals and governments are regulated by laws and not by arbitrary actions. No person or group is above the law.
- Taking responsibility for oneself and one's family — Getting a job, taking care of one's family and working hard in keeping with one's abilities are important Canadian values. Work contributes to personal dignity and self-respect, and to Canada's prosperity.
- Serving on a jury — When called to do so, you are legally required to serve. Serving on a jury is a responsibility that makes the justice system work, as it depends on impartial juries made up of citizens.
- Voting in elections — The right to vote comes with a responsibility to vote in federal, provincial or territorial, and local elections.
- Helping others in the community — Millions of volunteers freely donate their time to help others without pay: helping people in need, assisting at your child's school, volunteering at a food bank or charity or encouraging newcomers to integrate.
- Protecting and enjoying our heritage and environment — Every citizen has a role to play in avoiding waste and pollution while protecting Canada's natural, cultural and architectural heritage

for future generations.

- Defending Canada — There is no compulsory military service in Canada. However, serving in the regular Canadian Forces (navy, army, and air force) is a noble way to contribute to Canada and an excellent career choice. By helping to protect your community, you follow in the footsteps of Canadians before you who made sacrifices in the service of our country.

Canada is known around the world as a strong and free country with kind, courteous, worldly, and fun-loving people. Canadians are proud of this unique identity and proud of the traditions that make our country great.

Canadians inherited the oldest continuous constitutional tradition in the world and our commitment to ordered liberty, free enterprise, and hard work in a rugged environment helped make Canada an incredibly prosperous and peaceful society.

Today, Canada boasts the world's richest middle class, according to a report published, ironically, in the New York Times. According to the Reputation Institute, Canada is the world's most admired country, and according to a Forbes business report, Canada is the best place in the world to start a new business.

Canada is a great place to live. Most important of all, Canada has an open and welcoming society; any newcomer is welcome to become a Canadian and build upon this great tradition, but they must first sign on to the rights and responsibilities of Canadian citizenship.

PLURALISM, NOT FAILED MULTICULTURALISM

In Trudeau's imaginary Canada, there is no dominant culture or common identity, just a series of distinct and often isolated cultural silos, all of equal standing, who happen to occupy the same geographic territory.

We are not a British and French country with a strong aboriginal roots. We are just a pan-cultural society. We're all here, side by side, with nothing in common. No one can judge what is good or what is bad.

This is official multiculturalism. The bizarre theory espouses that a society like Canada has no identity and is instead made up of hundreds of diverse communities of equal national standing.

This fuzzy thinking postulates that Canada is not a country of French- and English-speaking people with western laws and traditions, but instead, a country that stands for nothing and allows everything.

State multiculturalism, as practiced in western European countries such as Belgium and the UK, employs a hands-off approach to integration and implies that all cultures in a society ought to receive equal standing. It prescribes that newcomers be able to join a new society without changing core aspects of their cultural practices, religion, norms or values, and assumes that a host society has no preference of one culture over another.

Cultural assimilation, by contrast, as practiced in the Arab world as well as such places as China and Pakistan, demands that everyone adopt one identity.

In these countries, the dominant norms, culture and religious practices of the host society must be accepted and practiced by all citizens, in many cases, upon pain of death. Many Muslim countries take this totalitarian approach to culture and religion, imposing archaic blasphemy and apostasy laws against those who reject or even criticize Islam.

Somewhere in between these two opposing theories lies the concept of cultural pluralism.

Religious pluralism encourages diverse groups and communities to engage and connect through shared respect, values and interest in one another. Similarly, cultural pluralism seeks to establish a primary set of norms and values that all citizens accept, thereby binding members of a society together.

Newcomers can maintain personal norms and values from their country of origin. They can enjoy a wide range of religious and cultural freedoms, so long as they accept the primary laws and norms established in the host society. Despite the Liberal fairytale of official multiculturalism, cultural pluralism far more accurately describes Canadian society.

The hackneyed and outdated Liberal brand of multiculturalism has been utterly refuted and dismissed in its other manifestations.

The European experience, based on terribly flawed immigration and integration policies, demonstrates conclusively that multiculturalism is a failed experiment.

Pluralism works a lot better in practice than the flawed approach of multiculturalism. In Canada, once this basic agreement to respect the rights and responsibilities of Canadian citizenship has been reached, Canadians of all backgrounds are free — even encouraged — to engage in diverse and distinct cultural practices.

It is through this shared foundation — a love and respect for Canada and for a free society — that various cultural communities connect and engage with one another.

Hindus, Sikhs and Muslims fight and kill one another in villages in India. Yet in Canada these communities are neighbours and friends.

The Middle East is plagued by hatred amongst Jews and Muslims who fight over territory and loathe one another's traditions. In Canada, by contrast, these two communities work very hard to engage one another and overcome their differences.

Canadian pluralism is distinctly different from failed European multiculturalism, a truth that former prime minister Stephen Harper rightly acknowledged and promoted.

As I wrote in an essay for C2C, Canada's conservative ideas journal, "Alongside immigration reforms, the Harper government has also subtly but substantially re-shaped 'official multiculturalism' as it was championed for decades by Liberal administrations. Unlike the failed multiculturalism of Europe — a hands-off approach that tiptoes around intolerance and tells newcomers they needn't change a thing; they can bring their own norms and laws to often supersede local customs — Canadian 'pluralism' as practiced by the Harper government focuses on integration. The immigration system accordingly favours immigrants who will likely succeed in Canada, in terms of language skills, economic prospects and compatibility, while also ensuring religious rights and freedoms are protected. In short, Canada selects immigrants who will say yes to both the Magna Carta and Masala Chai.

"A perfect example of the shift from multiculturalism to cultural pluralism is the revised Citizenship Guide for newcomers to Canada. The original guide was an ode to the Laurentian vision of Canada; it included multiple pages on the CBC and the importance of recycling, but never once mentioned Canada's military. The Harper government, led by former immigration minister [Jason] Kenney, revamped the guide to include and celebrate Canadian history — including its military history — and to emphasize traditional community and family values. The guide doesn't mince words; it unequivocally denounces ethnocultural practices such as female genital mutilation as 'barbaric', and stresses the need to abide by Canadian laws."

Interestingly, when the revised Citizenship Guide for newcomers was released in 2011, Justin Trudeau was the Liberals' immigration critic.[6] Not surprisingly, he took issue with a government document telling new immigrants that "Canada's openness and generosity do not extend to barbaric cultural practices that tolerate spousal abuse, 'honour killings', female genital mutilation, forced marriage and other gender-based violence." Trudeau found this objectionable, and said the government should make an "attempt at responsible neutrality."

He later retracted his comments and insisted he was not defending these barbaric practices. Trudeau learned his lesson about telling us what he really thinks. And we learned that Trudeau's impulse is to tiptoe around illiberal traditions and remain "neutral" when newcomers beat their wives or kill their daughters for the crime of embracing western values.

It's no surprise, then, that the Trudeau government has already said it will bring back the old Liberal citizenship guide, whitewashed of our western history and traditions and crammed full of mouldy leftist myths. Trudeau's Immigration Minister John McCallum complained about this citizenship guide, saying it is "a little heavy on the War of 1812 and barbaric cultural practices."[7] Who cares about Canadian culture or one of the defining events in our country's history, anyway?

Here is a column I wrote on Canadian pluralism and tolerance for the Toronto Sun, just days after Daesh terrorist attack and mass murder of civilians in Paris.

Canada is a Shining Example of Tolerance
November 20, 2015

It has been a difficult week around the world. The news has been dominated by bombings, mass murder, terrorism — both foiled plots and successful ones — and a backlash of xenophobia and racism in the wake of the Paris attacks.

Amidst all the horrible images on our television screens and in our newspapers, however, there is still reason for hope and optimism. That reason is Canada.

In a small city in Ontario, an unfortunate incident of intolerance quickly turned into a shining example of what makes our country so great. Just one day after radical Islamic terrorists attacked Paris, a mosque in Peterborough was torched. The arson attack caused some $80,000 worth of damage and left 1,000 people in the Muslim community without a place to pray. That is, until the Jewish community opened its doors.

When the Beth Israel Synagogue learned about the hate crime, its leaders offered members of the Muslim community a place to pray. The Jewish leaders, alongside a Christian group that also shares this space, worked with their Muslim counterparts to set up a fundraising initiative that has reportedly raised more than $110,000 to help repair the Masjid Al-Salaam mosque.

While Muslims are at war with Christians and Jews in other parts of the world, in Canada these religious communities co-exist. Even more so, they work together. According to Kenzu Abdella, the president of the targeted mosque and the Kawartha Muslim Religious Association, these three religious communities regularly hold open houses, engage in joint inter-faith dinners and participate in one another's celebrations. The Muslim community has prayed at this synagogue before.

This proactive engagement is part of the reason Canada is such a peaceful and cohesive society. Pluralism works in Canada. Of course, this experience is not unique to the faith communities of Peterborough.

Despite the very strained relationship between Syria and Israel, in Vancouver, a Jewish congregation has taken action to help Syrian refugees. Rabbi Dan Moskovitz asked his congregation at Temple Sholom for donations to help sponsor a Syrian refugee family. Within just a few days, they raised $40,000 — more than enough to support a family of four for an entire year.

In the Toronto suburb of Thornhill, Jews and Muslims are neighbours and friends. In fact, the Jaffari Islamic Centre and its next-door neighbour Temple Har Zion actually share a parking lot. These two communities share more than just a slab of concrete. They cooperate in a number of shared initiatives, from garage sales, to open houses, shared prayer services, panel discussions and anti-racism activism. During Toronto's annual Mosaic Interfaith Out of the Cold Program, the two congregations work together with nearly a dozen other religious communities and organizations to help those in need. This Jaffari Islamic Centre and Temple Har Zion have been living peacefully and sharing land for more than 30 years.

Similarly, in Richmond, B.C., there is a three-kilometre stretch of road dubbed the "Highway to Heaven." It is home to more than 20 religious schools and institutions built side by side. In this Vancouver suburb, members of the Sikh, Hindu, Buddhist, Christian, Jewish and Muslim communities gather and pray next to one another and work together to promote open dialogue. The "Highway to Heaven" has been called the most diverse concentration of faith groups in the world; it offers a living example of how different religious communities and ethnic groups can live in peace and harmony.

Here in Canada, we have an admirable example of religious tolerance and pluralism that should serve as a model for the rest of the world. This is just one more reason to love Canada.

WHEN A CANADIAN ISN'T A CANADIAN (ISN'T A CANADIAN)

> "A country, after all, is not something you build as the pharaohs built the pyramids, and then leave standing to defy eternity. A country is something that is built every day out of certain basic shared values."
>
> – Pierre Trudeau

We shouldn't worry too much about Justin Trudeau's wrongheaded thinking on Canadian identity. He was simply stealing a line from his late father, Pierre Trudeau.

Trudeau Senior, Canada's 15th prime minister, had a hand in rewriting Canada's history and entrenching new laws and institutions to reflect his own vision of Canada. Most notably, he established a codified charter, separating Canada from others in the British tradition which avoid written charters and the troubles that can arise from interpreting it.

Pierre Trudeau also introduced the concepts of official bilingualism and state-led multiculturalism, and promoted a pan-Canadian identity — efforts which were severely undermined by his economic mismanagement and centralization of power in Ottawa.

Trudeau the Elder distained the idea of the rowdy Canadian — an outdoorsman who works with his hands, loves sports and the wilderness, and enjoys a spirited and perhaps boorish night out with the lads. Instead, Trudeau Senior sought to wash the country of its folksy character; to erase Canada's blue-collar culture and instead perpetuate a myth that Canada was a young and cultureless society. It was untrue, but Trudeau ignored Canada's greater history and attempted to change its national character.

Fortunately, this didn't work. One doesn't have to journey too far from downtown Toronto, Ottawa or Montreal, to find the real character of our nation: an independent but community-oriented, hard-working but fun-loving, prudent yet jovial, responsible, religious, family-oriented nation with big hearts and open minds.

Trudeau shuddered at the image of the unruly Canadian, and instead tried to remake the country into his preferred image that reflects the educated collectivist European, more satisfied talking about the struggles of the working man in a café while sipping a glass of white wine, than the image of an actual working man using his back to earn a living.

Trudeau Junior certainly hasn't thought it through like his father.
Pierre Trudeau, while being possessed of an unsavoury arrogance, an affinity for Mussolini and fascism as a young man, and a love for Cuba and China, two of the world's most repressive socialist regimes, was also a thoughtful and accomplished man.[8]

He studied at Harvard, wrote long essays about public life in Canada and gave considerable thought to the policies he championed. Pierre Trudeau was a scholar, an author, an activist and a visionary.

Justin Trudeau, by contrast, spent his 20s and 30s having a good ole time. He travelled the world (and visited 90 countries, as he told a group of Persian community leaders, much to their bewilderment), smoked marijuana, enrolled in several university degree programs and did odd jobs, including stints as a snowboarding instructor, night club bouncer and actor. In his three-year teaching career, he taught junior school French at a tony private school and served as back-up drama teacher. Not exactly the trajectory of a man positioned to redefine our national identity.

A perfect example of Justin Trudeau's lack of thoughtfulness when it comes to Canadian identity was his blunder on the campaign trail, when he blurted out that terrorists should get to keep their Canadian citizenship.

Trudeau was giving a speech in Winnipeg and digressed into quoting an imagined Conservative attack ad declaring he was soft on terrorism. Trudeau said, "the Liberal Party believes that terrorists should get to keep their Canadian citizenship." The reason? "Because I do."

Trudeau then uttered his infamous line, that he believes "a Canadian is a Canadian is a Canadian."

Since then, however, Trudeau has failed to make the case for what it means to be Canadian and failed to properly define his idea of citizenship.

His concept of citizenship, and his now often-repeated line that "a

Canadian is a Canadian is a Canadian" is flat out wrong. It does not reflect Canada's long tradition of citizenship, either in law or in practice.

Canada is a country defined by how we live, not by how we look. We have always been a diverse and pluralistic society, one that does not meet the traditional definition of a nation. We are not a race of people and our country is by no means homogeneous.

Being Canadian does not imply any one ethnic background or ancestry, but is, even according to Justin Trudeau in his New York Times interview, a chosen identity based on shared values.

If being Canadian is an ascribed identity, rather than an absolute one, then his statement falls flat. To Trudeau, a Canadian isn't defined by the characteristics that make up a traditional nation of people or homogeneous societies, and yet, it is also somehow inalienable? It can't be both.

It is true that a Swede is a Swede is a Swede; since Swedes are defined by ethnic lineage, a common language and cultural ties. A Swede will always be Swedish, no matter where he or she lives. It is in their blood and their genealogy. That's because Sweden is a homogeneous society; the country is named after both the nation of people and the state that governs them.

This same logic can be applied to Japan, Somalia, Iceland, and many other homogeneous nation-states. A family could leave South Korea and live in Los Angeles for generations and still be Korean. That's because a Korean is a Korean is a Korean, regardless of factors such as where they live, other languages they may speak and what religion they practice.

But this logic does not extend to heterogeneous and pluralistic societies such as Canada, the U.S., Australia and New Zealand. And our citizenship laws reflect that.

Most countries around the world extend citizenship through blood. You are German if your parents are German. That is why the country still considers third-generation Turks to be "foreigners" on national census documents. Being born in Germany does not make one a German. Only being born to German parents makes you a German.

Canada and the U.S. take a different approach. We hand out citizenship to those born on our soil. You are Canadian if you are born in Canada, or if you emigrate and go through the necessary steps of acquiring citizenship. You do not automatically pass down Canadian citizenship if you have children outside of Canada.

For example, if a Canadian couple moved to Australia and had a family there, those children would be eligible for Canadian citizenship, but they would not be born with it. At some point in their lives, they would have to come back to Canada and go through the process of acquiring citizenship.

If those children declined to go through those steps, and never chose to live in Canada, they would not be Canadian. Their children — the grandchildren of the Canadians — would no longer be eligible for automatic Canadian citizenship. If they wanted to be Canadian, they would have to go through the same migration process as someone with no ties to Canada.

Far from an inalienable right, Canadian citizenship is a privilege, and our laws reflect that. Trudeau fails to grasp these basic facts of citizenship.

Trudeau himself said that Canadian identity is defined by our commitment to our country and our shared values.

Using Trudeau's own logic, a person who rejects these shared values, a person who joins our enemy and wages war against Canada, should no longer be part of our civil society. They have betrayed their commitment and therefore severed ties with Canada and Canadians. Their values bear no resemblance to those championed in a free society. Their choices show their deep disloyalty to Canada. Following Trudeau's logic, these people are not Canadian. No matter how many times Trudeau repeats his favourite line.

During his speech in Winnipeg, Trudeau went on to say he thinks it's "very scary" that the government gets to decide who can be a Canadian citizen if you were born in another country.

It's an odd statement. Who else, aside from the government, should determine who is a citizen? Should we leave these decisions to Wayne Gretzky? Or perhaps Jian Ghomeshi?

Since the Citizenship Act of 1946 was passed, millions have come to

Canada from other countries and been granted citizenship. Thousands of those have had their citizenship revoked, by federal governments of all stripes – including Liberals. If a person is found to have fraudulently obtained his or her citizenship, using fake documents or lying about their past, the government has a legal process by which it can strip citizenship. This was nothing new under the Harper government.

Jason Kenney, the former immigration minister, personally ordered over 3,000 citizenship revocations in just a few years. When Trudeau was asked about stripping away citizenship for war criminals or those who lied on their application to come to Canada, he said he was fine with that.

The Conservatives' Bill C-24 — the one Trudeau was criticizing before that crowd in Winnipeg — merely amended this act to allow citizenship revocation for serious crimes against Canada.

Under the bill, those convicted — found guilty in court — of terrorism, treason or espionage, those found guilty of taking up arms and fighting against Canada, can be stripped of their citizenship. Why does Justin Trudeau find that problematic? War criminals and liars are bad and should not get to keep their citizenship, but convicted terrorists deserve inalienable citizenship rights?

It didn't take Trudeau very long after he was elected to introduce his own changes, to reverse the Conservatives' citizenship bill.

Among the proposed amendments included in the Liberals' Bill C-6, the Trudeau government will no longer revoke the citizenship of those convicted of terrorism, espionage or treason.

Trudeau also announced that his government will reinstate the citizenship of the Jordanian terrorist who had his citizenship revoked under the Harper government.

Zakaria Amara was convicted of terrorism and given a life sentence back in 2010. As the ringleader of the Toronto 18, Amara pleaded guilty to charges of participating in a terrorist group and intending to cause an explosion for the benefit of a terrorist group. He was sentenced to life imprisonment.

Since Amara was born in Jordan, and only became a Canadian citizen as a young adult, the Harper government revoked his citizenship and announced he would be deported back to Jordan whenever he is released from prison. Thanks to Canada's revolving-door prison system, Amara is already eligible for parole in 2016.

But the Liberal government has other plans. It is not only saying this man can stay in Canada, but it is also honouring him with citizenship. I wonder if the Trudeau government will send a citizenship judge into Amara's prison cell to host a citizenship ceremony? Will he be asked to utter the oath of citizenship and pledge allegiance to Canada and the Queen? Maybe Trudeau will show up for a selfie.

This is a mockery of our citizenship. The Trudeau government is going out of its way to grant citizenship to a person who, judging by his actions, hates Canada and wants to kill Canadians.

We are bestowing the privilege and honour of Canadian citizenship upon a radicalized self-confessed Islamist terrorist who conspired to wage war against Canada. This lowlife terrorist does not deserve the privilege of being Canadian.

And yes, Canadian citizenship is a privilege, not a right.

Immigration Minister John McCallum justified the move by saying, "Canadian citizens are equal under the law." But that too is simply not the case. In Canada, much like every other western country, a person convicted of an indictable offence loses many of the rights and privileges that come along with citizenship. Serious criminals are no longer equal under the law.

Amara committed the modern-day equivalent of high treason. He should not be treated equally to law-abiding Canadian citizens.
When Amara is released from prison, we should be showing him the door, not handing him citizenship papers. Trudeau's policy sends a mixed message to jihadists and sets a dangerous precedent for Canada.

When a person decides to take up arms against Canada, committing treason or orchestrating a terrorist plot to kill Canadians, that person has forfeited his rights and freedoms. He has decided for himself that he no longer wants to be Canadian.

Giving back a known terrorist his citizenship does not increase the value of our citizenship. It devalues it. If a murderous Islamic terrorist, a convicted Jordanian jihadi, can be called a Canadian, then being a Canadian does not mean what it should.

The ability to strip such individuals of their citizenship sends a clear message to would-be terrorists. It tells them that Canada is not a safe haven for terrorism. It tells them that we take a no-nonsense approach to both our citizenship and national security. Contrary to Trudeau's rhetoric, this strengthens the value of Canadian citizenship.

Our Proud and Forgotten History

Despite the Trudeau family's limited vision of our country, Canada has a long and proud history. Many Canadians forget that Canada once played a strong and important role on the world stage, both militarily and as a moral leader.

The Trudeau legacy of whitewashing our history to perpetuate mouldy leftist myths deserves to be challenged. Justin Trudeau himself could benefit from reading up on Canada's history before he goes around the world denying it.

I won't hold my breath waiting for Justin to visit the Canadian history and archives section of the Library of Parliament , but I do know that all Canadians can benefit from hearing and reading more about the proud moments in our country's past.

Here is a collection of a few important and often ignored stories from Canadian history.[9]

In 1604, the first European settlement north of Florida was established by French settlers in present-day Maine and then Acadia, or present-day Nova Scotia. Contrary to popular lore, the European explorers collaborated and traded with the local aboriginal people, who themselves had migrated across the Bering land bridge from Asia centuries earlier.

The French and the aboriginals worked together to build a vast fur-trade network, and developed the early economy of the region. Soon, the English too were settling across the territory and forming strong alliances and trade partnerships with various aboriginal tribes.

In the 1700s, France and Great Britain battled for control of North America and, after the British defeated the French in the Battle of the Plains of Abraham near Quebec City in 1757, Great Britain renamed the French colony the Province of Quebec, and guaranteed religious and language accommodations.

Interestingly, British North America, later to be renamed Canada, was an early host to a large population of refugees. In 1776, when the 13 British colonies south of Quebec declared their independence, from the British, more than 40,000 people fled the American Revolution. These migrants, who were loyal to the Crown and therefore dubbed "loyalists," settled primarily in Quebec, Ontario and Nova Scotia.

Joseph Brant led thousands of loyalist Mohawk Indians into Canada, and came alongside British, Dutch, German, Scandinavian, aboriginal and others of diverse religious backgrounds including Jewish, Quaker, Catholic, Baptist, Methodist, Anglican and many others. Approximately 3,000 black loyalists — both freedman and slaves — came north seeking a better life and more freedom in Canada.

A few years later, in 1793, Upper Canada became the first province in the British Empire to move towards the abolition of slavery. Slavery has existed all over the world, in Asia, Africa, the Middle East, Europe and the Americas, and is still practiced in parts of Asia and notably by Daesh in Iraq and Syria.

Some of the first anti-slavery activists and reformers were Canadian. In 1807, the British Parliament prohibited the buying and selling of slaves, and in 1833 slavery was abolished throughout the empire. Thereafter, thousands of slaves fled the United States, followed "the North Star" and settled in Canada via the Christian anti-slavery network known as the Underground Railroad.

Canada's proud history and traditions continued, as many Canadians fought alongside the British Empire to defeat Napoleon's imperialist crusade across Europe.

Our American neighbours resented the British dominance on the high seas, and its interference with their shipping, and therefore decided to invade and take over Canada. In June 1812, the Americans launched an invasion against Canada, and quickly learned it would be no easy task to conquer their northern neighbours.

Canadian volunteer soldiers, including French and aboriginals, supported the British soldiers in defence of a sovereign and free Canada. In the 1813 battle at Chateauguay, 460 mostly French-Canadian soldiers defeated more than 4,000 American invaders near Montreal.

The Americans burned down Canada's Government House and the parliament buildings in York (now Toronto). In retaliation, Maj.-Gen. Robert Ross led an expedition from Nova Scotia to Washington, D.C., where in 1814, they burned down the White House, Capitol Building, the Library of Congress and several other government buildings.

Francis Scott Key was an American lawyer who was being held captive by the British in Baltimore and witnessed the bombardment of Fort McHenry. Following his release, Key was relieved to see the American flag still flying over the fort, and wrote a poem called the Star Spangled Banner. The poem was later set to the music of a popular English drinking song, "To Anacreon in Heaven," and was eventually adopted as the U.S. national anthem.

> "And the rocket's red glare
> the bombs bursting in air,
> Gave proof through the night
> that our flag was still there."

The Americans learned their lesson, as Canada proudly stood up for its sovereignty and independence, and fought for freedom against foreign control.

Canada won the War of 1812, which ensured that Canada would remain a sovereign nation, independent from the United States. Every time Americans sing their national anthem, whether they want to or not, they are paying tribute to Canada's military might.

Canada's military tradition continued, as most Canadians felt a close affinity to the British Empire and sought to support its gallant efforts. More than 7,000 Canadians, for instance, volunteered to fight in the Boer War in South Africa from 1899 to 1902. My great-grandfather, Ernest Malcolm of Vancouver, having lied about his age to appear old enough to be deployed, was one of those volunteers.

With the outbreak of the First World War in 1914, more than 600,000 Canadians volunteered for service out of a population of eight million.

Ottawa formed the Canadian Expeditionary Force, later renamed the Canadian Corps.

On the battlefield, Canadians earned a reputation as tough and hard-working soldiers. The horrific reality of trench warfare set in. More than 60,000 Canadians were killed in the war, including my great-grandfather who was well into his 30s when he volunteered again despite his wife's protests, and was shot in the battle of Ypres in Belgium in 1915.

Another notable soldier in this war was Pte. Bukkan Singh, the first Sikh man to enlist with the Canadian Armed Forces. Singh, who was born in India in 1893 and arrived in Canada in 1907, served in France and Belgium and was wounded twice in two separate battles. He was awarded war medals and returned to Ontario where he died of his injuries in 1919.[10]

Diversity in the Royal Armed Forces was not limited to Canadian Sikhs. In fact, 400,000 Muslim soldiers fought for Britain during this war, primarily in India. While the outcome of an agreement between the Brits (primarily T.E. Lawrence, better known as Lawrence of Arabia) and the Arabs is one of sad and mutual betrayal, the Arab Revolt against the Ottoman Empire helped destabilize the Central Powers and secure Great Britain's ultimate victory.

Despite the catastrophic and tragic loss of life — one in 10 Canadian soldiers died and one in three were wounded — Canada secured its steadfast relationship with the British Empire and a prominent reputation as innovative strategists, loyal and reliable allies and tough-as-nails soldiers.

Canadians played a pivotal role in the war, perhaps most notably in the Battle of Vimy Ridge, a German stronghold taken by the Canadian Corps in April 1917. Canadian skill and bravery led to the resounding success at Vimy Ridge, and is considered a major turning point in WWI, and was a defining moment in our national history.

The legacy of Canadians at Vimy Ridge brought great pride to our young country. The war strengthened national pride, particularly amongst English-Canadians and those with strong ties to the British Empire.

The Second World War further cemented Canada's bravery and resolve in the face of fascism. More than one million Canadians served in this war, and more than 44,000 were killed in battle in both Europe and Asia.

The Royal Canadian Air Force took part in the Battle of Britain and proved itself a world-class outfit with top-notch pilots and fighters. Canada contributed more to the Allied air efforts than any other Commonwealth country, with more than 130,000 air crew. Canadians also fought and suffered losses in the unsuccessful defence of Hong Kong in 1941 from attacks by Imperial Japan, and in the failed raid on Nazi-controlled Dieppe on the coast of France in 1942.

Canada's proud military history may embarrass the Trudeau administration, enough to remove it from Canada our citizenship guide, but it should be a source of pride to all Canadians.

Despite the best efforts of the Trudeau family, Canada's steadfast commitment to a free society will prevail.

The strength of our Canadian identity outlasted 16 years of meddling by Pierre Trudeau. We'll surely survive another reign by his handsome but vain, vacuous, and intellectually-stilted son.

Like his father, Justin Trudeau carries an unsubstantiated and false perception of this country. Justin is wrong to say that Canada has no core identity. He would be wise to pick up a history book and familiarize himself with the tremendous sacrifices made by early Canadians and the significant commitments they had to the ancient liberties born out of our western tradition. Maybe he'd learn a little about Canada's identity, which, after all, is derived in part from these early Canadians — the founding pioneers of our great country.

---

[1] "Trudeau campaign forced to address 2010 comments on Alberta," CBC News, Nov. 22, 2012. http://www.cbc.ca/news/politics/trudeau-campaign-forced-to-address-2010-comments-on-alberta-1.1241750

[2] Trudeau's Canada, Again. New York Times, Dec. 8, 2015. http://www.nytimes.com/2015/12/13/magazine/trudeaus-canada-again.html?_r=0

[3] American liberals, too, have co-opted this word, while liberals in Australia, New Zealand and Europe still believe in restricting government power in order to ensure greater individual rights and freedoms. I would likely have

been in Liberal in Canada prior to the Pearson and Trudeau bastardization of the movement, party and word.

[4] Bravo to the Harper Conservatives, specifically former citizenship and immigration minister Jason Kenney and his staff, including Dorchester Review founder and editor Dr. Chris Champion for updating the Canadian citizenship guide, Discover Canada, to reflect Canada's proud history, including its military history, which was intentionally ignored and left out by previous Liberal administrations.

[5] "Discover Canada Study Guide: The Rights and Responsibilities of Canadian Citizenship." Her Majesty the Queen in Right of Canada, represented by the Minister of Citizenship and Immigration Canada, 2012. http://www.cic.gc.ca/english/pdf/pub/discover.pdf

[6] "Trudeau retracts 'barbaric' remarks," CBC, March 15, 2011. http://www.cbc.ca/news/politics/trudeau-retracts-barbaric-remarks-1.985386

[7] "Liberals move to overhaul rules on revoking, granting citizenship," CBC News. Feb 25, 2016. http://www.cbc.ca/news/politics/john-mccallum-citizenship-act-repeal-bill-1.3463471

[8] "Young Trudeau: Fascist, anti-Semite, and separatist," Ottawa Citizen. May 31, 2006. http://www.canada.com/ottawacitizen/news/story.html?id=0c1b3dca-544a-45d8-8ce3-f577f9cb43a6

[9] While this section seeks to outline and highlight some of the high points in Canada's pre-Trudeau history, it is by no means a comprehensive historical analysis or account of the development of Canada. For those interested in a more thorough account, I recommend the books of Conrad Black, documentaries by John Robson and Brigitte Pellarin, or Chris Champion's monthly journal, The Dorchester Review.

[10] "Bukkan Singh remembered as 1st Sikh to fight for Canada," CBC News. Nov. 11, 2015. http://www.cbc.ca/news/canada/kitchener-waterloo/bukkan-singh-sikh-canada-veteran-first-world-war-buried-kitchener-1.3313795

CHAPTER 4: REMAKING CANADA

Manipulating Immigration for Political Gain

No politician can define or redefine the character of our nation. And no politician can invent or reinvent our national identity.

But politicians and sitting governments do get to set our immigration policies, which, over time, change the makeup of the country.

Smart migration policy is a delicate balance of: selecting good people, maintaining the right mix of migration categories and working hard to integrate newcomers into the economy and civil society.

The problem in Canada is that these important decisions are left in the hands of blundering politicians and partisan lackeys.

Politics is a game of numbers. From day 1 in office, politicians are thinking of ways to build coalitions, make inroads, maintain power and win the next election. Immigration is a tempting tool to use to grow a coalition and win future elections.

Justin Trudeau is taking political manipulation of our immigration system to a new extreme. During an incredibly dangerous period in world history, Trudeau is being smug and reckless.

Trudeau is making the wrong choices for Canada and implementing immigration policies that will have a profoundly negative impact. And he is doing it all for political gain.

In Canada, consider the sheer number of newcomers Trudeau has chosen to admit. In 2016, Canada will welcome 300,000 newcomers as permanent residents, and another 150,000 or more as temporary foreign workers and students. Canada will welcome more than 450,000 new residents this year — more than one per cent of our total population. We are adding a city the size of Victoria, B.C., or London, Ontario, every single year.

Depending on where they settle and how quickly they become citizens, it could also mean adding two or three new Members of Parliament.

Over the course of Justin Trudeau's four-year term in office, Canada plans to admit at least 1.2 million new immigrants — more like 1.5 million if you consider that many students will transition from student visas to permanent resident status, while many temporary foreign workers find a way to become citizens.

Canada will settle more people than the current population of Manitoba by the time Trudeau is up for re-election and likely the equivalent of the population of New Brunswick, P.E.I., and Newfoundland and Labrador combined. That's like adding anywhere between 14 and 27 seats to the House of Commons.

If Trudeau wins a second term, he will have selected and resettled at least three million people — the population of Montreal or all of Alberta. That is enough new voters to swing just about any election.

Trudeau's Liberal Party machine — the people who gave us the sponsorship scandal and canceled the gas plants in Ontario — will be working relentlessly to ensure that as many of these newcomers as possible are card-carrying (or at least voting) Liberals.

The Liberals also use immigration policy to play favourites with ethnic communities in key ridings, with targeted bells and whistles. The strategy is well underway. It was evident from Day 1 in Trudeau's mandate.

Immediately after winning office, the Trudeau government introduced a flood of irresponsible changes to Canada's citizenship and immigration laws, part of the Liberals' ambitious agenda to change what it means to be Canadian. Within its first six months, the government had already introduced legislation and enacted cabinet orders to:

- Restore Canadian citizenship to convicted terrorists who were dual citizens.
- Bring 50,000 refugees into Canada through a flawed federal sponsorship program rather than partnering with the more successful volunteer refugee sponsorship programs.
- Eliminate language testing for Canadian citizenship for anyone aged over 54, handing out Canadian passports to people who have made no attempt to learn English or French.
- Cut the amount of time someone must live in Canada before qualifying for citizenship down to just three years — part-time — further opening our immigration system to fraud and abuse.
- And, increase the number of newcomers admitted into Canada annually; adding more spots for elderly senior immigrants while cutting economic immigrants — those who come to Canada and create jobs.

Each of these policies is dangerous in its own right. Taken together, they will have devastating consequences for Canada.

These decisions are not being made out of naivety or good intentions. These are not clumsy mistakes. These policies are deliberately engineered for partisan gain.

The Liberals think they are being clever. They believe these little "tweaks" to our immigration system will go unnoticed or unreported by a complicit media establishment and a distracted public. They think they can manipulate the immigration process to build their election coalition and get away with it.

The Liberals' Machiavellian approach to immigration will almost certainly backfire, either for Canada socially and economically, or for the Liberals politically.

Politicians take for granted that Canadians are generous and welcoming people. Most assume that the anti-immigration sentiment that lives deep in the hearts of Europeans could never spread into Canada.

Yes. It is true that there are no anti-immigration parties in Canada, with the exception of the separatist Parti Quebecois. Even the PQ is distancing itself from its 2013 secular "charter of values." PQ leader Pierre-Karl Peladeau has refused a meeting with France's anti-immigration presidential candidate Marine Le Pen.

But events across the globe are having an impact on the way Canadians view immigration.

Canada has among the highest proportion of foreign-born residents and citizens in the world, in part because we have historically supported broad immigration. Canadians understand the important role immigration can play in economic growth.

But this support has its limits.

Canadians will support high levels of immigration only if they believe immigration will help build a better country. And Canadians are starting to have serious doubt about whether immigration does, in fact, build a better country.

Ipsos Global conducts annual polling on immigration attitudes around the world. In 2006, this survey found that 75 per cent of Canadians believed that immigration was a good influence on the country. This overwhelming support was unmatched in other western countries.

Compare this, at the time, with immigration support levels at 54 per cent in Australia, 52 per cent in the United States, and 43 per cent in Britain.[1]

It's remarkable that Canadians in 2006 were nearly twice as likely to favour immigration as their counterparts in Britain or the U.S.

Politicians took advantage of that willingness to welcome and accept large-scale migration, but failed to make a sustained effort to persuade Canadians of the benefits of immigration.

Fast-forward a decade later, and a 2015 Ipsos poll found that only 37 per cent of Canadians thought immigration has a positive impact on our country.

Since 2006, Canadian public opinion has become much more in tune with other English-speaking western liberal democracies. Canada's 37 per cent is in line with 36 per cent in Australia, 28 per cent in Britain, and 25 per cent in the U.S.[2] Likewise, only 43 per cent of Canadians say immigration has been good for our economy.

While support for immigration has fallen across all western liberal democracies, it has plummeted in Canada, dropping nearly 40 percentage points in less than a decade. It's an unprecedented shift in public opinion, one that should make our politicians sit up and take notice.

There are plenty of reasons why such a drop in public opinion might occur: a slumping economy, rising global terrorism, a perception of fraud and abuse in the system, increased local crime rates, welfare dependency attributed to immigrant communities and so on.

A lot has changed in the world since 2006. Watching Europe fracture and slump under the weight of its immigration mismanagement has also contributed to a change of heart among many Canadians.

We cannot solely point the blame at politicians for the change in public opinion, but we can point out that most politicians have not acknowledged this shift, least of all Justin Trudeau.

And in implementing his hidden agenda, Trudeau risks driving even more Canadians away from accepting further immigration. His policy changes will contribute to growing public sentiment that mass migration is a bad deal for Canada. Unbeknownst to Trudeau, his policies could be fueling an anti-immigration backlash similar to the ones rocking the U.S. and Europe.

There is a case to be made for an open approach to immigration — to help boost the economy and grow our country. It can be particularly helpful in bringing in skilled young workers to address problems arising from Canada's aging population. (For more information on that problem, see my book Generation Screwed).

While there are many economic and moral reasons to embrace sensible immigration, the Trudeau government is not persuasively making this case. Instead, is it arrogantly throwing the doors open and demanding that we accept the tectonic changes being imposed.

The Ipsos polling echoes other studies and similar findings. Canadians are losing their trust in open migration, and the Trudeau Liberals are totally out of touch with the trajectory of opinions and perspectives of everyday Canadians.

Justin Trudeau is playing a dangerous game with the most delicate aspects of Canada's identity, security and prosperity.

Trudeau's barrage of changes will hurt Canada in four key ways: it will undo Canada's "gold standard" immigration system and the economic benefits this brings; it will undermine our national security and public safety, thereby making Canada more vulnerable to criminal networks and the menace of radical Islamic terrorism; it will open us up to fraud and abuse from those who seek to take advantage of Canada's generosity; and it will steadily undermine public trust, driving more Canadians to reject immigration.

Trudeau's reckless, thoughtless, careless immigration scheme will worsen the growing uneasiness towards immigration. Eventually, it may lead to Canada closing its doors to the world.

A Dangerous Approach to Resettlement

Canada has long enjoyed a reputation as having one of the world's most effective immigration systems. Over time, Canada devised a strategy that worked.

But our world is changing and just because these policies survived the 20th century does not mean they work today. We must constantly learn from our mistakes, and the mistakes of others, to devise the best strategy for Canada.

Canadians are already nervous about national security: they want to see new measures taken to strengthen our citizenship and immigration rules. Instead, the Trudeau government is taking the opposite approach. It is intentionally ignoring legitimate concerns and brazenly putting its own partisan interests ahead of proven security measures.

Consider Trudeau's Syrian refugee pledge, a perfect example of the government's haphazard approach. Trudeau's original campaign pledge was to welcome 25,000 Syrians, in the space of two months, through the federal government's assisted refugee program.

When it comes to sponsoring refugees into Canada, there are two parallel programs that can be used: private — or volunteer — sponsorship and government-led sponsorship.

Trudeau wanted the whole program to be administered by Citizenship and Immigration bureaucrats and government-funded resettlement agencies, without tapping into the private volunteer sector. It was Trudeau's own government-funded agencies which asked the government for a "pause" in accepting new refugees because they were so overwhelmed.

And while the government-sponsorship side was struggling to keep its head above water, the corresponding private sponsorship refugee program was under-utilized and offering to do more.

In Canada, charities, churches and families can raise funds and directly sponsor refugees. Instead of relying on the depleted resources of the government, privately sponsored refugees rely on their hosts to teach them English, help them find a place to live and get started in Canada.

More than just helping bear the load of responsibility with the government-led refugee program, the private sponsorship program has empirically proven to be the better program.

Direct social interaction — the human hand of friendship extended by a sponsor, rather than a government agency — has a very positive effect on refugees.

Statistics from the Department of Citizenship and Immigration Canada show that privately sponsored refugees do much better financially than their government-sponsored counterparts. During their first year in Canada, private-sponsored refugees reported lower unemployment levels than the Canadian average. And after five years in Canada, only about 15 per cent of private-sponsored refugees relied on social assistance, compared to 30 per cent of government-sponsored refugees.

And yet, for political reasons, the Trudeau government refuses to use the private refugee program to its full capacity. Although Trudeau finally allowed some private sponsors to help with the Syrian program, most will still be admitted through the government-sponsored program. Fewer than one-third will be privately sponsored.

That's because Trudeau prefers using the federal government and taxpayer dollars to provide a service, even when individual Canadians have proven they can do a better job.

Canadians have shown that they sincerely want to help. They want to provide more than just their tax dollars funneled through an inefficient bureaucracy; they raise money through their churches and charities, volunteer their time and effort and they personally welcome Syrian newcomers into their communities. Instead, the federal government is standing in their way.

Trudeau is sending money and work to the people who helped him get elected, the union leaders and the immigration activists who dislike the very existence of a private refugee system. He is ignoring the many Canadian communities and churches who are willing to help and have proven themselves better able to provide support and assistance to refugees.

Trudeau's partisan and narrow-minded approach is doing Syrian newcomers no favours. Thanks to Trudeau's mismanagement, the plight of Syrian refugees continues even after they arrive in Canada. Far from being rescued from harsh conditions and uncertainty upon arrival, a string of media reports shed light on the ongoing difficulties these newcomers face once here.

The CBC interviewed a Syrian mother, Zaneb Abu-Rukti, who spoke through a translator from a Toronto hotel room where her family had been abandoned for several weeks. "Our kids don't have anywhere to play, nowhere to go out," she said. "We feel like we're just trapped in a prison."

According to volunteers, some of these refugees are actually trying to return to the Middle East. Refugees who were carefully selected, vetted and flown to Canada at a significant cost to taxpayers, then wanted to pack up and go back to refugee camps in Lebanon and Jordan. Abu-Rukti said her family received more help while living in those camps than they've received here in Canada.

During the 2015 election campaign, Justin Trudeau told Canadians that Syrian refugees needed to be immediately evacuated from the Middle East. We were told Canada's best contribution to the ongoing conflict in Syria was to open our borders and allow refugees to come here. But after interacting with the federal government in Canada, some of these refugees say they'd prefer to return to the camps. That is a slap in the face to the Trudeau policy.

A CTV report revealed that 600 government-sponsored Syrian refugees, long after their arrival, were crammed into a budget hotel in Toronto with little support or communication, and were desperately waiting to move into permanent housing.

In Edmonton, Global News reported that a large number of refugees arriving in Canada were "acutely ill". Local hospitals struggled to cope with the needs of many patients arriving in Canada with illnesses picked up abroad. According to an internal memo, a flu outbreak had "paralyzed" Alberta's refugee resettlement agencies.

This is what happens when you insist on putting political interests ahead of the best interests of Canadians. You put Canadian public health at risk. You leave refugees stranded. And worst of all, you risk creating persistent integration problems that could threaten Canadian society. Refugee resettlement is a complicated business. Just as important as being properly screened and vetted, these newcomers need to be properly welcomed.

Newcomers need to be supported by a community that can teach them the language, tell them about our culture, help them find a place to live and assist them in securing meaningful employment. Communities tend to be better at this than government bureaucrats and contractors. And yet, this debacle was caused by Trudeau's preference for government-sponsored refugees over private sponsorship.

This is an example of Trudeau's partisan interests trumping Canada's best interest. He rewards his friends and government agencies rather than using a refugee resettlement approach — private sponsorship by volunteers — that has proven to be better at providing services to newcomers.

The Trudeau government's early refugee blunders will have long-term consequences. Our resettlement of Syrian refugees could be a true Canadian success story. Instead, for families like Abu-Rukti, the Syrian mother desperately trying to give her kids a better life in Canada, Justin Trudeau has made them feel isolated and abandoned.

True Patriot Love

Trudeau's wild opening salvo has been to throw open our doors to as many as 50,000 Syrian migrants, plucked from an active sectarian war zone and global training ground for radical Islamic terrorism.

He then insisted on using an inferior government-sponsorship program to resettle these migrants into Canada. This is just the beginning of the inept and self-interested immigration strategy his government has in store for Canadians.

In his first six months in office, the Liberals have drastically altered each of the four components of good migration policies — selection, composition, levels and integration — without making any adaptations to meet the security challenges of the 21st century.

Immigration Minister John McCallum said it best when he told reporters in early 2016 that his government was introducing "radical changes" to Canada's citizenship laws. But his government has never made the case that Canada's immigration laws were in need of changes, let alone radical ones.

Canada's citizenship rules were once held up as the gold standard among western liberal democracies. We were already the best of the best.

So unless the focus were on further cracking down on fraud and boosting economic migration — two approaches taken by the Harper Conservatives — why make radical changes at all? The Liberals have yet to articulate their rationale, so we can only assume it is partisan in nature.

McCallum eventually tried to explain his thinking. "We are, in general, trying to reduce the barriers people have to overcome to become a citizen," he said in an interview. In other words, the Liberals want to make it as easy as possible to give away Canadian citizenship. And Bill C-6, the legislation tabled by the Trudeau government during its first session in Parliament, is transparent in its naked political motive.

The Liberals want to increase the number of newcomers welcomed to Canada each year. They want to use generous migration policies to woo voters in selected electoral districts with high concentrations of recent immigrants. And they want to fast-track newcomers' ability to gain

Canadian citizenship so they can vote in the next election. This is all part of a plan of creating one million new Liberal voters in time for the next federal election.

Prior to the introduction of Bill C-6, any permanent resident wishing to become a Canadian citizen was required to meet a set of criteria, or "barriers," to use McCallum's jargon, in order to transition from permanent resident to citizen.

Applicants were required to live in Canada, and file annual tax returns to the federal government. They were required to understand the rights and responsibilities that come along with being Canadian, and pass a written test on Canadian citizenship. And, if the person was under the age of 65, he was required to pass a straightforward language test to show he spoke and understood basic English or French, as the case may be.

These are common-sense measures and are more than fair. The vast majority of Canadians agree that becoming a citizen is a privilege, not a right. Gaining Canadian citizenship is not supposed to be easy.

By overcoming these "barriers" — living in Canada, learning our language and passing the citizenship test — newcomers demonstrate their commitment to our country. Meeting these straightforward citizenship tasks is more than a symbolic gesture; it shows a sincere desire to join the Canadian family.

Newcomers work hard to gain their citizenship, and in turn, they feel a sense of pride and accomplishment in meeting these requirements; it helps to develop loyalty and a love for Canada.

During this process of qualifying for citizenship, newcomers show they are committed to Canada, they demonstrate patriotism and love for Canada and they learn about what it means to be Canadian. Each step is also an important component in Canada's integration strategy.

Removing these so-called barriers — making it easier for newcomers to become citizens with no effort — is a disservice to both newcomers and to Canadians.

Newcomers expect the process of moving to a new country to be challenging. If it wasn't hard, everyone would do it. If we start waiving these requirements, we are sending a mixed and dangerous message to newcomers. We are telling them that integrating is optional and learning our language is unnecessary.

Heck, you don't even need to live in Canada, pay taxes or contribute to our country if you don't want to.

Just don't forget to show up on election day and vote Liberal.

After spending a few weeks teasing out their radical changes, the Liberals finally introduced Bill C-6.[3] Among other things, this bill amends the Citizenship Act as follows:

1. It removes the government's ability to revoke the citizenship of convicted terrorists, traitors and those who have taken up arms against our Canadian Forces in the field;
2. It eliminates the requirement that applicants pledge that they actually want to live in Canada;
3. It reduces the amount of time an immigrant has to live in Canada before becoming a citizen; and
4. It gets rid of the requirement that immigrants over the age of 54 learn English or French, or know anything about Canada's history.

In one fell swoop, the Liberals are radically changing what it means to be Canadian. And they are doing it for all for their own political gain.

Quick and Easy Citizenship

During the election campaign Justin Trudeau said he would scrap the Conservatives' Strengthening Canadian Citizenship Act, also known as Bill C-24, so the government could no longer revoke the citizenship of dual citizens convicted of terrorism.

Trudeau, we remember, repeatedly parroted his election talking point "a Canadian is a Canadian is a Canadian."

In Trudeau's world view, "a Canadian is a Canadian is a Canadian," even if, for example, they have burned their passport and travelled overseas to fight for Daesh or al-Qaeda.

Trudeau's stance weakens the value of Canadian citizenship, it lends credibility to the notion that Canada is soft on terrorism and a safe haven for criminal networks. It's a wrongheaded policy, but at least Trudeau was straightforward about it during the election campaign.

The "radical changes" McCallum introduced in Bill C-6, however, were not part of the Liberal election platform. In fact, they were never mentioned on the campaign trail.

Instead, the Trudeau government, without pointing to any research or making the case that our citizenship process is overly burdensome, is rewriting the laws to open Canada up to quick and easy citizenship.

As reckless as handing out citizenship to terrorists, the other aspects of Bill C-6 are just as worrisome and will affect the way that millions of people will soon acquire Canadian passports.

First, the Liberals are reducing the amount of time it takes for a newcomer to qualify for citizenship to just three years, living in Canada part time. Far from making a great sacrifice and demonstrating one's commitment to Canada, under the new Trudeau laws, a newcomer must show only a casual interest in Canada.

Likewise, the Liberals are removing a pledge that newcomers commit to living in Canada after acquiring citizenship.

This was never a legally binding agreement, but rather an aspirational commitment to live in Canada, serve the new country and contribute to the tax base in some way or another. But even this symbolic pledge to Canada is apparently too much of an imposition. Committing to Canada is just too much to ask, according to the Trudeau Liberals.

The most egregious aspect of this new bill is the elimination of the language requirement for anyone over the age of 54. The Liberals made some attempts to justify this disastrous and unnecessary change, but once again, their spin was unconvincing and contradictory.

Liberal MP Shaun Chen tried to make the case that the policy was merely aimed at helping elderly seniors.

"Often times, families are sponsoring elders and grandparents at a very elderly age. It's very challenging and difficult for them to be at such a high proficiency of English or French," said Chen.

But his argument falls flat when you look at the Citizenship Act. The law already allows an exception for elderly immigrants. Anyone over the age of 65 does not need to pass a language test in order to become a Canadian.

The Liberal changes to the citizenship law lower the language test exemption from age 65 down to just 54. Since it takes four or five years for newcomers to qualify for citizenship, down to just three under the new rules, this means that people who come to Canada in their late 40s will no longer be required to learn French or English.

Even worse, there will be nothing stopping someone coming to Canada in their 20s or 30s and simply waiting to turn 54 to apply for Canadian citizenship. We shouldn't be fooled into thinking the language change is just for elderly seniors. The Liberal government's proposed bill is primarily aimed at those who are middle-aged and working-aged.

The Liberals are pandering to a small minority in ethnic communities in Canada who want quick citizenship and easy access to Canada's generous social services and benefits.

They are catering to newcomers who don't want to learn our language and don't want to integrate into Canadian society, but instead, simply want all the benefits of Canadian citizenship. The Trudeau government is putting Canada's successful immigration and integration policies at risk to score political points with a small minority of immigration activists, consultants and lawyers. It's a cheap political trick and one that will create long-term problems in Canada.

Since Canada has had its own citizenship, we have required newcomers to learn basic English or French. We don't expect them to enjoy reading Margaret Atwood (who does?) but there has always been an expectation that newcomers learn our language.

The law, as it stands today, requires those under the age of 65 wishing to become a Canadian citizen to pass a basic language test. New Canadians should be able to communicate with their neighbours, go to a store to buy food, or speak to an emergency room doctor in English or French.

This language requirement has served Canada well. We have a

harmonious and peaceful society, where newcomers strive to join the Canadian family and Canadians are gracious and welcoming. We do not have extensive isolated ethnic silos that police avoid. We don't have entire generations of people born in Canada who never integrate.

For a country that spends $2.4 billion annually trying to teach English-Canadians French and French-Canadians English, it's bizarre that the government would suddenly tell newcomers not to bother learning either. For a man whose father was the architect and mastermind of official bilingualism in Canada — a program of which I am critical — it is sad to see Justin Trudeau abandon this aspect of Canadian citizenship and identity to cater to some activists and special interest groups.

Some immigrants don't want to learn English, or want to spare their parents the struggle of integrating. If Justin Trudeau had any courage, he would say "too bad." Instead, he is caving to these migrants and weakening our Canadian identity.

We know that when people are not required to learn our language their employment prospects drop significantly. There is no greater qualifier for economic success in Canada than having a grasp of the local language. That should be on the very first page of the citizenship guide we hand out to newcomers. It should simply say: learn English, learn English, learn English. Or Etudiez le français, étudiez le français, étudiez le français. Learn our language, and you will massively increase your chances of success in Canada.

Instead, here we have the Liberals telling working-aged migrants that learning our language is optional and even discouraging them from trying. Trudeau's policy encourages older migrants to come to Canada, to not bother learning our language or getting a job, but to enjoy a long retirement while living off of the services provided by hard-working taxpayers.

This policy reduces the barriers that keep out free-riders and fraudsters who seek only to take advantage of our generosity. In fact, it directly invites these free-riders to apply to come to Canada.

Not only does this policy undermine our economic interests, it also adds to the security concerns already prevalent throughout Europe.

When we don't ask immigrants to learn our language, we drive them away from mainstream Canada and leave them isolated in closed ethnic communities, like the neighbourhood in Belgium that sheltered the terrorist mastermind of the Paris massacre and Brussels bombing.

Toronto-area Liberal MP Gary Anandasangaree argues that this is already happening.

"Many Canadians may not be able to pass that test either," he said of the language test.

If so, that is both astonishing and troubling. But unlike this MP, Canadians shouldn't shrug their shoulders and accept that we have isolated immigrant communities, then adopt lax laws to make the problem worse. We should take the opposite approach and encourage ethnic communities to branch out and engage with the broader community in Canada, in English or French.

Many Canadians will be left scratching their heads and wondering why the new government decided to overhaul our citizenship guidelines in the first place. The system was not broken, it was not unnecessarily burdensome and, if anything, it still left Canada open to the many scammers, fraudsters and criminal networks looking to take advantage of our generosity.

So why make it easier to gain access to Canadian citizenship, and all the privileges, benefits and entitlements that come along with it? The answer is simple. Politics.

It is clear that the Liberals are in a rush to turn newly arriving immigrants into voting citizens. They want to make things easier for newcomers, in order to win votes and lifelong political allegiances.

They are catering to the demands of political activists, consultants and lawyers who want an easy path to Canadian citizenship.

A small number of newcomers in some ethnic communities want to sponsor elderly family members into Canada and give them a quick path to citizenship so they can then benefit from free health care and social welfare programs.

This is a special interest group like any other. They encourage their broader communities to vote for the politicians who promise the most freebies and giveaways.

The Trudeau government is going out of its way to pander to these free-riders.

By reducing the barriers to citizenship — by handing out Canadian passports after just three years and to people who don't speak a word of English or French — the Liberal government is trying to appeal to a small but politically powerful subset of Canadians in ethnic communities. They are enticing these voters with easy citizenship and quick access to Canada's vast social welfare programs.

And they're doing it all in time for the next election. The Liberals are putting bad politics ahead of good policy. They are putting newcomers and foreigners ahead of Canadian citizens and taxpayers. And they are putting the interests of the Liberal Party — their own naked political ambitions — ahead of the national interest.

Undoing the Canadian Advantage

Canada has long championed the model of aligning our immigration system with promoting economic growth and filling gaps in the labour market.

The Harper government focused meticulously on cracking down on fraud and abuse in the system. But it also fast-tracked the process for newcomers with critical job skills, where employers desperately needed them to move projects ahead and put Canadians to work.

The Chrétien Liberals before them were also focused on boosting economic migration. Canada pioneered a "points system" to help the government select the candidates that possess the skills proven to make newcomers successful in Canada. This tool was very effective when used properly.

Our immigration system awards points for various personal attributes and accomplishments. Once you surpass a certain threshold of points, you have the opportunity for a fast-tracked visa. This allows us to use a scientific and evidence-based method for selection. Canada awards points for the attributes our society needs and qualities that lead to success in Canada. For instance, with an aging population, decades of declining fertility rates among Canadians and retiring baby boomers, Canada is in great need of young workers. Canada can therefore award extra points for migrants in their 20s and 30s, and fewer points to older migrants.

As labour market trends change, often before university admissions officers can react, our points system allows for a nimble reaction to skills shortages in the economy.

Canada used to look for doctors and health care professionals through our immigration system. But in 2016 it no longer makes sense to import foreign-trained doctors when Canada has a deep pool of talent, as well as some of the best medical schools and training facilities in the world. We do, however, need computer programmers and mechanical engineers for our expanding tech sector.

Until recently, our immigration system was centered around recruiting the most talented immigrants with the skills and abilities our country needs. Canada also gives points for those who speak English or French, those who are university educated, and to people who have specific skills and training in areas where there are typically lots of jobs, for instance carpenters, electricians and cooks.

The CNN host, former editor of Foreign Affairs and former Time Magazine editor-in-chief Fareed Zakaria noted in 2012,[4]

> "Canadian immigration policy is now centered on recruiting talented immigrants with abilities the country needs. Those individuals can apply for work visas themselves; they don't even need to have an employer. The Canadian government awards points toward the visa, with extra points for science education, technical skills and work experience.
>
> The results of the system are evident in Vancouver, where American high-technology companies like Microsoft have large research laboratories and offices. The people working in these offices are almost all foreign graduates of American universities who could not get work visas in the U.S. They moved a few hours north to Vancouver, where they live in a city much like those on the American West Coast. Except, of course, that they will pay taxes, file patents, make inventions and hire people in Canada.

> Sixty-two per cent of permanent-resident visas in Canada are based on skills, while the remainder are for family unification. In the U.S., the situation is almost exactly the reverse: two-thirds of America's immigrants enter through family unification, while only 13 per cent of green cards are granted because of talent, merit and work. And it's actually gotten worse over time. The cap on applications for H1-B–visas (for highly skilled immigrants) has dropped in half over the past decade."

Zakaria dedicated an entire episode of his CNN show GPS to exploring Canada's immigration system and discussing what the U.S. can learn from our successful approach to migration policies. On Twitter, Zakaria said that, "Canada has the most successful set of immigration policies in the world." He wrote in a Time magazine article that America "is losing the best and brightest" to Canada and that "Canada is one nation that's getting immigration right."

Zakaria painted an extraordinarily rosy picture of Canada's migration policies. While his praise is certainly welcome, he also stumbled through some technical aspects of our immigration process and overlooked many of the tensions that exist in our system.

For instance, 62 per cent of our immigration intake may be to those with "economic category" permanent residency spots, but that does not mean that 62 per cent of our visas are based on "skills." Right off the bat, more than half of the economic category visas are given to the immediate family members of the primary applicant.

Only about one in every four immigrants to Canada is selected for economic reasons.

Furthermore, just because someone comes to Canada under the economic category, that does not make them a skilled worker.

A significant portion of these visas are distributed through the Provincial Nominee Program (PNP), under which provinces get set numbers of spots to sponsor workers to live and work in their province.

There are many problems with PNP, including fraud and abuse in provincial investor programs, but a major flaw is also that these programs often do not bring in skilled workers. Many of the workers who come to Canada under PNP end up working low-skilled jobs at factories and fast food restaurants.

Suffice it to say, Canada's immigration system has never been perfect. Zakaria is absolutely correct, however, in emphasizing the importance of economic migration and getting the right mix of newcomers.

Both Europe and the U.S. allow family reunification to dominate their immigration system, and it's become a significant problem for them.

When economic considerations are not weighed in during selection of newcomers, countries inevitably bring in migrants who are unskilled and unlikely to contribute to the economy.

This causes even more long-term problems as migrants become dependent on social welfare, draining the host government of cash and creating resentment among the host population. It perpetuates any perception that immigrants are simply free-riders and taking advantage of the system.

Getting the right mix of immigrants is essential. Ideally, Canada would welcome 80 per cent of its immigrants through various economic categories and the remaining 20 per cent via refugees and family reunification. Canada has an historic and humanitarian obligation to help those in need of asylum, which is why about 10 per cent of our migration should be reserved for refugees.

Likewise, when a Canadian goes abroad and gets married, they should be able to sponsor their spouse and their spouse's dependent children for citizenship.

Family reunification should be limited to spouses and children. Instead, and for crass political purposes, Canada has also created a family reunification category for the parents and grandparents of immigrants. This is the exact opposite goal of boosting our economy and reversing an aging population.

Bringing elderly immigrants into Canada and allowing them full access to government-run health care and welfare is both wrong and unaffordable.

It is unfair to force Canadians who have worked and paid taxes for 40 years to wait in a health care queue behind an immigrant who has never worked or paid taxes here. This is not a bigoted complaint, but one based on justice and fairness. And math.

Super Visa

In the 1990s, the Liberals became notorious for opening Canada up to welcome tens of thousands of elderly seniors per year. This reached a record high of 42,742 elderly parents and grandparents in 1993.[5] The Conservatives made changes to the system, placing a pause on new applicants for instance, but they did not have the political courage to eliminate the program altogether.

The Conservatives actually increased the number of parents and grandparents in 2013 to nearly double its 2012 number in an attempt to reduce the backlog, while placing a pause on new applicants. Even this move was condemned by hyper-activists on the left and the powerful collection of immigration consultants, agencies and lawyers.

One of the most innovative tools implemented by the Harper government was a new visa that allowed parents and grandparents to quickly and easily come to Canada. Rather than applying for permanent residency, and waiting several years in a queue, parents and grandparents were able to apply for a 10-year multiple-entry visa, known as a "super visa."

Under this visa, immigrant seniors could come and go as they pleased and stay in Canada for up to two years at a time. The only major difference between the super visa and permanent residency is that these elders needed to purchase private health insurance.

This is only fair, since they didn't work in Canada and did not pay Canadian taxes. Most countries require that foreigners and visitors purchase private health insurance; when I studied in Australia, I was required to purchase health insurance as a condition to receive my student visa.

The super visa policy was both fair and compassionate to elderly parents and grandparents. Since there was no backlog, applicants received their super visa within just a few weeks, rather than the seven-year average it took for permanent residency. Most elderly seniors do not want to free ride and rip off Canadian taxpayers. They are more than happy to purchase their own insurance and not receive handouts in Canada. It was a win-win policy.

There were, of course, some angry voices who claimed this was unfair. They wanted more elderly parents and grandparents from their community to have a free ride in Canada.

When Trudeau took over, his immigration minister McCallum announced the government would drastically restructure the composition of the immigrants Canada welcomes. Prominent liberals such as Fareed Zakaria had praised the existing focus on economic immigration. Nonetheless, the Trudeau government cut economic immigration, tripled the number of refugees Canada accepts and increased "family reunification" by 12,000 spots.

McCallum said his plan represents a "significant shift in immigration policy towards reuniting more families." But once again, the Liberals are not being upfront with Canadians about their plan.

As mentioned earlier, when someone receives an economic visa to come to Canada, they can automatically sponsor their immediate family members — a spouse and any dependent children. Family members make up over 60 per cent of all economic immigration. In order words, our economic category of immigration already encompasses family sponsorship.

The "family reunification" category is different, and more than one-third of family reunification spots are dedicated to bringing in elderly parents and grandparents.

The Trudeau government's "shift" is a mere ploy designed to enable elderly parents and grandparents to receive Canadian welfare, health care and eventually qualify for OAS, GIS and other social programs in Canada. The Liberals will get more votes, and young taxpayers will get stuck with the bill.

Justin Trudeau and company are reversing every bit of progress made by the Harper Conservatives on immigration reform in pursuit of a political agenda.

Rather than letting parents and grandparents come to Canada only through the super visa, the Liberals are appeasing the angry voices in some immigrant communities and allowing more elderly seniors to become permanent residents. This will give more elderly foreign seniors access to the social benefits earned by Canadians through a lifetime of work and taxation. It will cost taxpayers untold billions.

We've seen this type of thinking from the federal Liberals before.

Back in 2009, Liberal MP Ruby Dhalla introduced a bill that would have allowed new immigrants to begin collecting OAS after just three years in Canada. While the Canada Pension Plan (CPP) is funded through a direct payroll tax and given only to those who contribute to the fund, OAS is funded through the federal government's general revenue and makes up about 16 per cent of all federal spending. It is means-tested, which means it is clawed back from wealthier seniors. OAS is only available to those who have been in Canada for at least 10 years.

Under Dhalla's proposed bill, that would have been knocked down to three years, allowing more people to gain access to this fund who had never paid taxes in Canada.

This proposal prompted immediate and obvious outrage from taxpayers across Canada. Thankfully, the bill never got anywhere in the House of Commons. It pandered to immigrants who want to sponsor their elderly parents into Canada, but don't want to be financially responsible for them.

Dhalla was catering to those who want a free ride, those who see Canada as an easy target.

While Ruby Dhalla is no longer a Liberal MP, her party is up to the same tricks. They are offering quick and easy access to Canadian citizenship, and all the benefits that come along with it, to elderly foreign seniors who will be a significant drain on our taxpayer-funded services.

The Trudeau Liberals are fixated on manipulating our immigration system to score cheap political points. And it's no different in 2016. They will once again be bribing some politically powerful newcomers with Canadian taxpayers' money. They will be putting our taxpayer-funded health care and retirement funds at risk in order to win future elections.

This is crass, old school, pork-barrel politics.

The Liberals are tossing aside the very stated purpose of sensible immigration policy: to boost economic growth and reverse the demographic tidal wave approaching Canada as baby boomers leave the workforce, stop paying taxes in a meaningful way and begin collecting expensive government services and benefits.

We can now add another 20,000 elderly immigrants per year to the pool of retired baby boomers. This will make the future for Canadian taxpayers, especially young taxpayers, even more burdensome. This ploy undermines economic immigration, and invites further skepticism that newcomers are just free-riders. No wonder so many Canadians no longer support immigration.

Canada: the World's Doormat

If the Trudeau government is going to admit a million newcomers every three years, the onus is on them to articulate why this will be a good policy for Canada, and how it will impact everyday Canadians. They must also convince us that these newcomers will become part of the Canadian family and accept mainstream Canadian values. So far, they've yet to even acknowledge this obligation.

When politicians purposely turn a blind eye to abuse and even welcome free-riders, fraudsters and scammers, Canadians start to look more skeptically at the immigration system. When Canadians see immigration hurting our economy or contributing to job losses, their support for broad immigration inevitably drops.

For instance, when the Royal Bank of Canada fired Canadian workers and replaced them with temporary foreign workers, Canadians were rightly upset.

It is likewise frustrating to see how Canada's Employment Insurance rules are at odds with its temporary foreign worker program.

Why are we paying unemployed workers to sit at home, but at the same time enabling companies to hire cheaper labour from developing countries? Writing in the National Post, Atlantic Director of the Canadian Taxpayers Federation Kevin Lacey elaborates on the contradictory policies.[6] Why are there 10,900 temporary foreign workers in Atlantic Canada when about 30,000 people in New Brunswick collect EI, he ponders. Why does the government allow companies to sponsor temporary foreign workers when 1.3 million citizens are unemployed? These policies do not build faith in the immigration system.

The temporary foreign worker program is broken, other programs are flat-out corrupt. A prime example of an immigration program rife with fraud and corruption is the Provincial Nomination Program (PNP), which allows provinces to directly sponsor workers to fill jobs vacancies. There are many problems with PNP. For starters, it contradicts the Charter of Rights and Freedoms, which grants freedom of mobility to everyone in Canada.

Telling a newcomer that they must live in Alberta restricts this freedom. So governments are unable to force visa-holders to stay in the sponsoring province, thereby making the visa — and the whole program — totally ineffective. Alberta can grant a visa to an immigrant but that immigrant can live wherever they like — and many end up in Vancouver and Toronto.

The PNP initiative, like the temporary foreign worker program, also makes little sense for provinces with high unemployment levels. Why, for instance, is Newfoundland able to bring in workers when it has a provincial unemployment rate of over 14 per cent, double the Canadian average? Provinces should focus on employing residents who are looking for jobs and discouraging people away from EI, rather than paying out unemployment benefits while helping corporations fill vacancies with foreign labour.

PNP is so corrupted, it occasionally provokes stories that sound like the plot of a Hollywood movie. P.E.I. had to shut down its investor program after taking millions of dollars from wealthy businessmen from Hong Kong and China. A backlog of more than 4,500 people paid upfront but were left waiting for their actual visas to be processed.

Ottawa called for an inquiry into its PNP program after bribery allegations surfaced and media reports alleged that a P.E.I. government bureaucrat accepted cash-stuffed envelopes while interviewing would-be migrants at a hotel in Hong Kong.[7]

Easily the worst example of rampant abuse, however, was the former federal Investor Immigration Program, and its continuing counterpart, the

Quebec Investor Immigration Program.

Under the federal scheme, an investor was able to give the Canadian government an $800,000 bond in exchange for citizenship. After just five years, the government would return the money, and a newcomer would have all the rights and privileges of Canadian citizenship. The only real cost to the newcomer was the interest that money could have earned in a savings account or in mutual funds. Hardly a sacrifice given recent interest rates.

This scheme helps explain the real estate frenzy in Vancouver. Wealthy Chinese investors were taking money out of China and using it to buy up the city's real estate.

According to the Economist, Vancouver is now the most expensive city in North America. It has the second-least affordable housing market in the world, after only Hong Kong.[8]

The average detached home in the city now sells for over $2.23 million.[9] The number gets much higher in the prestigious west side of Vancouver, where old, neglected and tear-down homes often cause bidding wars amongst wealthy Chinese investors. They don't like the look of those old Canadian homes — better if they can just tear them down and build their own dream homes.

A 2014 report from the Department of Citizenship and Immigration Canada provides more insight into just how bad of a deal this program really was. Not only did immigrant investors drive up the cost of real estate, buying homes that often sit empty, they've also failed to contribute much to the economy.

The study found after 10 years in Canada, these millionaire investors paid only a fraction of the taxes their net worth would suggest.[10]

After 10 years in Canada, the average immigrant who came through this investor program had a taxable salary of only $15,800.

One in three immigrant investors did not file a tax return at all — claiming zero income in Canada.

After a decade, these millionaire investors paid on average only $1,400 in annual taxes.

By contrast, the average immigrant who came through the skilled worker program earned $46,800 per year and paid $10,900 in annual income taxes. The average Canadian pays about $7,500 in annual income taxes.

Only a small fraction of these foreign investors actually start companies in Canada. Only 10 per cent report any self-business activity and, the ones that do, are dominated by real estate rentals and ownership.

Of the immigrant investors who do start businesses, 63 per cent are in real estate.

Far from being a boon to our economy and creating jobs, these so-called investors are actually a drain on our social system.

Another study, this one from the University of British Columbia, shows that many of these investor immigrants are actually draining government coffers rather than contributing. The report highlights the low incomes and possible welfare dependency among those living in Vancouver's exclusive neighbourhoods.

According to Stats Canada, upwards of 30 per cent of adults in upscale Vancouver neighbourhoods report poverty-level incomes.

Neighbourhoods where homes typically sell in the $2 million to $6 million range also have the lowest reported incomes in the city.

You can imagine why.

Under the immigrant investor program, a typical scenario may include a wealthy businessman from Hong Kong who buys a house in cash, then sends his wife and children to live in Canada, while he remains in Hong Kong. Since no one is earning any income in Canada — no one is contributing to the tax base — these families qualified for and received welfare, despite living in multi-million-dollar homes and likely living like millionaires.

Our taxes are buying their champagne and caviar.

And don't forget, they use Canada's free health care and education, without paying taxes.

Meanwhile, a real estate gold rush among wealthy Chinese investors has driven home ownership out of reach for the vast majority of Vancouverites. This undermines the social contract we rely on, and rightly invokes anger and frustration.

The federal cash-for-passports scheme was finally put to an end by the Harper government in 2012, but the Quebec program is still going strong and admitting thousands of so-called investors each year.

Some 200,000 "investors" have been admitted through this program in the past two decades. Around 60 per cent of the immigrant investors from each of these programs end up living in B.C., and more specifically Vancouver.

The immigrant investor program has made lawyers rich, caused a real estate gold rush and driven home ownership out of reach for everyday people in Vancouver.

The immigration lobby protested heavily when Harper shut down the program, and immigration lawyers are likely lobbying the Trudeau government heavily to have it set up again. It's how they make their money.

The Trudeau government would be wise to refrain from re-opening this can of worms.

Government schemes tend to attract opportunists and fraudsters, and it is therefore the government's job to block them

Governments must devise policies to safeguard against those who seek to take advantage of our generosity and get a free ride in Canada.

Here is a final example where the Harper government made changes to protect taxpayers from foreign fraud rings, one that the Trudeau government instantly dismantled.

Within the first few months in office, the Trudeau government quietly killed a Conservative law that limited the ability of bogus refugees to drag out their deportation process by launching appeal after appeal.

When someone arrives in Canada and declares himself or herself a refugee, they must prove they are truly in need of Canada's help.

In order to determine if a person is a bona fide refugee, he or she is given a lawyer and sent in front of a judge from the Immigration and Refugee Board of Canada (IRB). If the judge rejects the claim, the individual can appeal the decision. The problem is that rejected refugee claimants could appeal and ask for reviews of their case five or six times. Many rejected asylum seekers managed to stay in Canada for years, even decades, dragging out the appeals process and wasting government resources.

As you can imagine, this was an expensive game of cat and mouse. According to a Canadian Border Services Agency report, the federal government spends $92 million annually on deportations. Furthermore, when a bogus refugee appeals their claim and uses countless court resources throughout the appeals process, these individuals are also given generous housing and welfare benefits. They are enrolled in the Interim Federal Health Program, which provides full access to Canada's health care system plus many benefits above and beyond what Canadian citizens receive.

The quagmire of a system invites people from around the world to take advantage of Canada's generosity, including human smuggling rings. That is why the Harper government made changes to it. Under the Harper government reforms, if an IRB judge determined that a landed asylum seeker was not a true refugee, in accordance with UN convention definitions, and the person came from a safe country such as France or the U.S, they were immediately deported. (Yes, Canada receives refugee applications from people from France and the U.S.) If the person came from an unsafe country, like Syria or Colombia, they would get to stay and appeal the decision.

Before the Harper government streamlined the refugee determination process, many would-be refugees arriving in Canada were not from China or Pakistan but from Hungary — a European country. In 2011, 4,453 Hungarians came to Canada claiming to be refugees. Only two per cent were found to be bona fide cases; the other 98 per cent of claims were either abandoned or rejected by the IRB. An assistant Hamilton crown attorney estimated that these fake refugees alone cost Canadian taxpayers $500 million per year.

In 2013, after Harper's common-sense reforms were implemented, only 96 people from Hungary claimed refugee status in Canada.

Harper's reforms saved taxpayers hundreds of millions of dollars. But the Trudeau government has different priorities.

They are less concerned with the soaring costs of government services, not to mention the perverse incentives for bogus refugees to come to Canada.

Instead, they are more concerned with guaranteeing Charter rights to foreigners and giving endless appeals to wannabe refugees from other western democracies.

The Liberals are trying to appeal to urban elites in downtown Toronto and Montreal who care more about getting praise from UN bureaucrats than working in the best interest of all Canadians.

They care more about appealing to immigration lawyers and special interest groups than about securing our borders and maintaining the integrity of our immigration system. Under the Liberal approach to immigration, Canada is no longer the world's gold standard; we are the world's doormat.

The Real Fear-Mongers

Justin Trudeau adamantly insists that "a Canadian is a Canadian is a Canadian," and that our citizenship is an inalienable right.

In his campaign to undo any and all changes introduced by the Harper Conservatives, he defends his government's radical and reckless agenda by insisting that Canadians rejected Harper's approach. But it was also the Liberals' intentional misrepresentation of Conservative policy that helped undo Harper's re-election campaign.

Trudeau accused the Conservatives of creating two tiers of Canadian citizenship; by stripping a handful of foreign-born convicted terrorists of their citizenship, Trudeau charged that all foreign-born and naturalized Canadians became second-class citizens.

Trudeau's Liberals simultaneously ran a vicious campaign, drumming up fear amongst immigrant communities and spinning that Harper's citizenship bill could ultimately be applied to all newcomers.

Many new Canadians honestly believed that the Conservatives' citizenship revocation for foreign-born terrorists could be levied against any foreign-born citizens who break any law. If you get a speeding ticket, make a mistake while filing taxes, or forget to return your library books, they feared, you could be deported and have your citizenship revoked.

This fear-mongering campaign, coupled with poor communication by Conservative spokespeople, helped Trudeau win office. Worse, it left the Conservative Party to deal with the worst accusations possible: of racism and bigotry. The Conservatives are the party that elected the first Muslim MP, the first Asian MP, the first Inuit MP and the most diverse cabinet in Canadian history, but somehow they were catapulted back in time and forced to defend these incredibly damaging accusations.

Far from making a principled and patriotic appeal to all Canadians, Trudeau's divisive mudslinging created division and mistrust between newcomers and Canadians.

Trudeau's campaign tricks may have turned many new Canadians against voting Conservative, but they also created general mistrust and caution amongst new Canadian communities. And most ironically, it is the Trudeau Liberals through their comprehensive immigration and citizenship reforms who are creating a separate class of citizens: Canadians of convenience.

Canadians of convenience are those who live abroad but keep a Canadian passport as an insurance policy.

These Canadians of convenience use their citizenship to send their children to Canadian universities and avoid paying international tuition fees. They may send a family member to Canada if they fall ill and want to take advantage of Canada's government healthcare.

But they are very unlikely to start a business in Canada, pay any taxes or volunteer in a local community.

Instead, these Canadians of convenience take advantage of our generosity and do not contribute to our society. They utilize public resources — schools, hospitals, roads and even welfare — and find ways to maximize the benefits for themselves.

They drive up the cost of living, launder money and buy homes with cash, and never bother to learn English or integrate into Canadian society. Instead, they form isolated communities, if they even bother setting foot in Canada at all. Many just let their mega-mansions sit empty and come to Canada only for an annual ski trip in Banff or Whistler.

These foreigners, who happen to hold Canadian passports, also pose a risk to Canada's public safety and national security. They are Canadians second, and their real loyalties lie elsewhere.

These Canadians of convenience are the real "first-class" citizens. You and I and every other law-abiding, tax-paying stooge in the country are the second-class citizens. We are forced to pay for the whole system, while the Trudeau government turns a blind eye and enables these schemes to flourish.

Rather than cracking down on these Canadians of convenience, Trudeau is purposely making things easier for them. He is intentionally and knowingly weakening the value of Canadian citizenship — because he never really valued it that much in the first place.

---

[1] "The plan to behead the prime minister," The Economist, http://www.economist.com/node/7036979?fsrc=scn/tw_ec/the_plan_to_behead_the_prime_minister

[2] Ipsos Global Immigration Survey: http://www.ipsos-na.com/news-polls/pressrelease.aspx?id=6930

[3] "An overview of proposed changes to the Citizenship Act." Government of Canada Backgrounder. http://news.gc.ca/web/article-en.do?nid=1036069&tp=930&_ga=1.54678060.64135688.1456533854

[4] "Broken and Obsolete," Fareed Zakaria. June 8, 2012. http://fareedzakaria.com/2012/06/08/broken-and-obsolete/

[5] Citizenship and Immigration Canada database. www.cic.gc.ca

[6] "Temporary foreign workers aren't the problem. Employment Insurance is," Kevin Lacey, Special to the National Post. July 8, 2014. http://news.nationalpost.com/full-comment/kevin-lacey-temporary-foreign-

workers-arent-the-problem-employment-insurance-is

[7] "Bribery alleged by PEI immigrant program workers," CBC News. Sept. 16, 2011. http://www.cbc.ca/news/canada/prince-edward-island/bribery-alleged-by-p-e-i-immigrant-program-workers-1.994038

[8] "In Vancouver, North America's most expensive city, rich Chinese take the blame for skyrocketing home prices," Financial Post. Oct. 7, 2015. http://business.financialpost.com/personal-finance/mortgages-real-estate/in-vancouver-north-americas-most-expensive-city-rich-chinese-take-the-blame-for-skyrocketing-home-prices

[9] *Ibid*

[10] "Evaluation of the Federal Business Immigration Program, Department of Citizenship and Immigration, Government of Canada. Oct. 25, 2014. http://www.cic.gc.ca/english/resources/evaluation/bip/08.asp

CHAPTER 5: GLORIOUS AND FREE?

Conclusion

Despite all its problems, Canada is well positioned to face the major challenges of the 21st century. Thanks in part to our geography, and in part to our traditions, Canada is an anchor of peace and stability in an increasingly chaotic and dysfunctional world. There is no better place to be than Canada, and it is the job of all Canadians to ensure that we remain a strong, steady and secure country.

Canada is also prepared and capable in the global war against radical Islam, thanks to the decisions made by Canadian leaders over the past several decades. But we are not immune to the problems brewing in Europe or the U.S. Let's compare our Canadian experience to what is going on south of the border.

In America, elites on both sides of the political aisle have, for years, failed to meaningfully address the country's broken immigration system, even exploiting the government's failures to score political points.

Meanwhile the growing problem of illegal immigration has intensified, creating anger and hostility among the American population.

Rather than taking action to fix the problem and addressing the legitimate concerns of the people, politicians squabbled with one another and presented solutions that were wildly out of touch with everyday citizens.

Both Democrats and Republicans tried to ignore the genuine concerns Americans have with illegal immigration, each hoping the other side would fix the problem or that the problem would self-correct or disappear. It didn't.

Instead, Americans began rallying around politicians representing viewpoints that were once considered extreme. On the one hand, millions began to support the only person to strongly condemn illegal immigration and the porous southern border with Mexico, and one of the few to challenge the narrative that Syrian refugees pose no threat to national security. On the other side, millions of Americans rallied behind a man who pledged to completely change America by allowing as many immigrants in as possible.

American political elites ignored the legitimate concerns of a broken immigration system. What they got in return is Donald Trump and Bernie Sanders.

Donald Trump calls for a complete halt to all immigration — a policy that would require the U.S. to spend billions of dollars to build walls, rip up trade agreements and execute the mass deportation of millions of people.

Bernie Sanders, by stark contrast, calls for virtually unlimited immigration to the U.S. Sanders wants to give citizenship to anyone who wants it, including millions of illegal immigrants.

For those not paying close attention, these radical developments seemingly came out of nowhere. Over the course of just a few months in 2015, the most extreme voices on both sides of the spectrum were catapulted into the centre of the political debate.

Suddenly, these extreme voices began to represent mainstream attitudes.

But the issue was years in the making. And now, as each side digs in its heels, a path forward becomes increasingly complicated and uncertain. This polarizing issue has created a volatile political culture that will continue to divide Americans for the foreseeable future. Immigration divides America. It makes America less secure. And continues to create real second-class citizens who live outside the system in their own parallel society.

Let this be a cautionary tale for Canada. If you ignore the problem of a broken immigration system for long enough, the problem will erupt in ways that no one can predict.

In Canada, Justin Trudeau is leading our country down this perilous path.

Trudeau is taking Canadian generosity for granted. He assumes, mistakenly, that Canadians fundamentally and overwhelmingly support all immigration, no matter the scale, no matter the composition, and no matter the time frame for integrating newcomers into our population.

Trudeau is implementing policies that will change the makeup of our country, dividing our society and putting future generations at risk.

He is moving forward with a scheme that will weaken the value of our Canadian citizenship. He is opening the door to fraud and abuse, not to mention jihadism and violence.

He is manipulating the system and playing partisan games.

As Canada continues to cope with some of the largest sustained immigration flows in our history, and as the world deals with the advancing threat of radical Islamic terrorism, we have to decide what kind of country we want to be.

Do we want to become like Germany, where there are third-generation immigrants who don't speak a word of German?

Do we want to become like France, where there are ethnic neighbourhoods police dare not enter?

Do we want to become like America, which wants to build physical walls to separate itself from the outside world?

Or, do we instead want a country with a consensus on immigration, where newcomers are expected to integrate into our society?

The key issues and challenges of migration policy in the 21st century have shifted. Our policies can no longer simply be aimed at bringing in as many people as possible to fill our country and boost economic growth.

Things needs to change in Canada, and national security must play a prominent role in our immigration decision-making.

Our leaders must prove to the public that mass migration will not undermine public safety or social cohesion. We must always remember, regardless of how uncomfortable or scary it may be, that there is an enemy is at our gate. We must always remain vigilant to the threat of violent extremism and the evolving ways our enemies wage their war.

In the past, Canada put national security and social unity ahead of special interests and free-riders. We took a generous and compassionate approach to migration, but we also asked that migration policies benefit Canada first and foremost.

Justin Trudeau takes the opposite approach.

His preference for putting newcomers ahead of Canadians, his callous disregard for taxpayers, and his reckless citizenship policies will have a lasting and destructive impact on Canada.

Trudeau may wake up in four years to a country that is polarized — a country where the majority of people reject any and all immigration, as many voters in Europe and the U.S. do in 2016. And he will only have himself and his party to blame.

Justin Trudeau was handed a peaceful country with a long tradition of responsible governance and welcoming immigration. And he is putting this enviable tradition at risk.

This is the real threat of Justin Trudeau's assault on Canadian citizenship. Unless he is stopped, it may well be his enduring legacy. He took a peaceful, tolerant and pluralistic country, strong and free, and turned it into a battleground.

ACKNOWLEDGEMENTS

This was a fun project, and I have many people to recognize. First, thank you to the fine folks at the Toronto Sun, and especially Adrianne Batra, for publishing my columns and giving me an amazing platform. Thanks also to Lorrie Goldstein and Anthony Furey for your mentoring and advice. And, of course, thank you to the loyal readers of the Toronto Sun. I love being a part of the paper.

Thank you to the wise Gregory Thomas, for your guidance and encouragement; to my editor Bruce Annan, a master of the English language; to Chris Matthew, for your tireless support; to my brother Fraser, the most sensible guy around; and to his high-school drama coach (and Canada's 23rd prime minister) for providing me with endless writing fodder.

Thanks to the Center for a Secure Free Society and the Canadian Global Affairs Institute for giving me a place to hang my hat.

Thanks to friends Mark Milke, Rikki Ratliff, Hamish Marshall, Ezra Levant, Chad Rogers, Joseph Humire, Fernando Menendez, Alejandro Chafuen and Ana Curic for your encouragement and in helping me work through some of the ideas of this book.

Thanks to my dad for listening to my wonky policy rants. Thanks to my mum and sister Brittany, for always helping me with everything, and to Amber, Drew, Maren, Gray, Asher, Alistair, Axel, Afton, Phaydra, Charlotte, Rachel, Susan, Kia, Katrina, Michael, Lulu and Dylan for your love and support.

Finally, thank you a hundred times to Maryam and Amir: for moving to Canada, for letting me into your lives, and raising a remarkable son and a true gentleman.

ABOUT THE AUTHOR

Candice Malcolm is a nationally-syndicated columnist with the Toronto Sun, a fellow with the Canadian Global Affairs Institute and an international fellow with the Center for a Secure Free Society in Washington, D.C. She is a former advisor to the minister of citizenship and immigration, former director of research at Sun News Network and was the director of the Canadian Taxpayer's Federation in Ontario.

Candice is the author of the book Generation Screwed, a free market analysis of public economics in Canada, which become a #1 best-seller in economics on Amazon.ca. Her nationally syndicated column in the Sun newspapers appears on Thursdays and Saturdays.

Born and raised in Vancouver, B.C., Candice is a ninth-generation Canadian and loves to travel. She has master's degrees in international relations and international law, and splits her time between Toronto, Vancouver and San Francisco, with her husband Kasra.

Made in the USA
Charleston, SC
06 May 2016